D0941569

CHABOT COLLEGE-HA

2 555 000 011616 W

# THE SORROW
# AND
# THE PITY

# THE SORROW AND THE PITY

**A FILM BY MARCEL OPHULS**

*Introduction by Stanley Hoffmann*

*Filmscript Translated by Mireille Johnston*

*Biographical and Appendix Material by Mireille Johnston*

*Outerbridge & Lazard, Inc.*
*New York*
*Distributed by E. P. Dutton & Co.*

Standard Book Number: 0-87690-080-5
Library of Congress Catalog Number: 72-87708
The film, "Le Chagrin et la Pitié," was originally copy-
righted © 1969 by Productions Télévision Rencontre S.A.
The English translation to the filmscript and all other text
material in this edition is copyright © 1972 by
Outerbridge & Lazard, Inc. Photographic material copyright
© 1972 by Productions Télévision Rencontre S.A.
First published in the United States of America in 1972
Printed in the United States of America

**Design: Samuel N. Antupit**

Grateful acknowledgment is made for permission to reprint
the following: "Notre espoir," by Maurice Chevalier and
"Ca fait d'excellents français," by Jean Boyer, Copyright
© 1941 and 1939 respectively by Editions Salabert; "Ca
sent si bon la France," Copyright 1942 des Publications
Francis Day S.A.; and "[Up on Top of a Rainbow]
Sweepin' the Clouds Away," by Sam Coslow (french title:
"J'veux ma place au soleil," by Battaille-Henri), Copyright
© 1930, U.S. copyright renewed 1957, reprinted by
permission of the publisher, Famous Music Corporation.

**Outerbridge & Lazard, Inc.**
**200 West 72 Street**
**New York City 10023**

# CONTENTS

## IN THE LOOKING GLASS

### I

Like all works of art that probe the truth about a society, *The Sorrow and the Pity* is a mirror presented by the authors to their audiences. How sharp a mirror a movie such as this one turns out to be, compared with novels or even with plays, not to mention memoirs or histories! The printed page, or words on a stage, are no substitutes for the faces, voices, gestures of "real" people. No written flashback has the power that explodes on the screen when a scene from 1940 and a scene from the present are juxtaposed, showing the same man at thirty years' distance. No narrative, no fictional reconstruction matches the newsreel or the live interview. Especially when the subject is nothing less than a nation's behavior in the darkest hour of its history, it isn't surprising that the reactions should be so passionate. In skillful hands of clever people, movies or television films can be formidable weapons.

The first group reflected in the mirror is today's audience. The reactions of American reviewers and spectators already tell us something about the troubled America of the early 1970s. The cruelties and frailties which this movie throws into our faces cannot be dismissed as mere evidence of French decadence or Nazi beastliness. We know now that the "banality of evil", self-deception, the thousand ways in which people deny or repress guilt so as to preserve or restore their self-esteem, are not just tales from abroad. The question which this movie raises for Americans is not: "Under similar circumstances, would we have behaved better?" It is: "Under different but not incomparable circumstances, have we behaved better?" *The Sorrow and the Pity* could be the title of a very similar documentary—on Americans and the Vietnam war. We all know American counterparts of every one of the human types who appear on the screen . . .

It is of course the reactions of the French of the early 1970s which are the most interesting. What do they tell us about France today? Their intensity shows that the time has not yet come when a probing attempt to come to terms with those gruesome years would be met with equanimity. The divisions among the French which this movie displays are still too deep. Any debate becomes a psychodrama. For almost thirty years, France has been flooded with memoirs, pamphlets, accounts of trials, charges and counter-charges, case studies, biographies, revelations, press reviews, concerning the years of Vichy and occupation. But there has been only one attempt to write an overall history[1] and it gained general acceptance only because of its blandness. Litvinov once said that no arbitration of conflicts between the USSR and capitalist countries was conceivable, because only an angel could be objective. Today, it is still impossible for a Frenchman to deal with that period without choosing his camp deliberately—or actually taking sides even if he hadn't wanted to. This movie underlines once more that the dividing lines were far from straight. Each side was an unstable and unhappy forced coalition. The supporters of Pétain were highly uncomfortable about those Frenchmen who took the old man's words too seriously, or too far, and, like Christian de la Mazière here, decided to fight under a German uniform. The Resistance was torn by the rivalry between the Communists and the non-Communists, by old suspicions between Left and Right, by differences of emphasis between those who in occupied France fought above all the Germans, and those who, in Vichy France (which wasn't occupied until November 1942), saw the reactionary regime of Pétain as their main foe. Nor was there ever perfect harmony between the Resistance in France and de Gaulle in London and Algiers. Moreover, as the movie so penetratingly shows, many people took refuge in the humble and often painful tasks of daily survival, and did their best (if that's the right word) to stay out of the battles and away from the heat. But, to paraphrase Paul Valéry, if mankind lasts because of the masses of people for whom enduring has a higher value than

---

1. *Robert Aron's* The Vichy Regime, *New York, 1958.*

acting, its fate is determined by those who choose, act and decide. And that minority—for it is always a minority—was split into two irreconcilable, if heterogeneous, groups. Their internal divergences were subordinated to one common goal: the liberation of France, on one side; accommodation to Nazi Germany (assumed, with enthusiasm or resignation, to be victorious or unbeatable) and concomitant antidemocratic reform, on the other side. Therefore, today, when one tries to write or to talk about those years, one cannot avoid making up one's mind; and such were the stakes, such was the depth of feeling, that any effort to be "fair" to each side usually annoys both and serves History no better than it helps reconciliation.

The movie by Marcel Ophuls and his associates does have a point of view: it is on the side of the Resistance. Obliquely—through cutting, and by putting them in highly embarrassing positions, and by extracting damning statements from them—it exposes the German ex-occupiers, and the officials of Vichy, such as Pétain's former Youth Minister, who has forgotten his "revolutionary" fervor of 1940, and of course Laval, whose rise to a kind of feudal lordship is unforgettably shown up by the very attempt of his son-in-law to get beneficiaries of Laval's special favors to testify to his goodness. If de la Mazière, of the French Waffen SS, is presented in a better light, it may be because he carried his convictions, however evil, to their logical conclusion, and was able to look back with candor (not untainted by complacency). The movie denounces Vichy's complicity in the anti-Semitic propaganda campaigns and, above all, in the deportation of Jews. As a result, the defenders of Vichy who are still around (including Laval's son-in-law) have vigorously criticized the movie and trotted out again the arguments that show that Vichy actually protected France from a worse fate, defended French Jews from extermination, and served as a sacrificial shield. Two points must be made about this. First, a coming study of a young American historian punctures those arguments item by item, and, on the basis of documents found in unpublished German and American archives, reveals that Vichy's interest in collaboration far exceeded the "necessities" of shielding France.[2]

2. *See the forthcoming book by Robert O. Paxton.*

Secondly, the protests of the Vichyites do not damage the case so vividly made by this movie: even if Vichy had saved France from, say, the fate of occupied Poland, even if Laval did his best to delay the arrest of French Jews, the moral price paid was horrendous; Vichy France made moral choices which no government should be willing to make—about which hostages should be shot (Communists), which Jews should be delivered (foreign ones, including children the Germans had not planned to grab). It lent the police, the judicial apparatus, the penitentiary administration, not to mention the controlled media of France to the Nazis, or used them (as in anti-resistance repression) for purposes that served the Nazi cause. Next to this, homilies about Pétain's good intentions, harangues about Laval's good deeds, hagglings about comparative results all wilt. But that is precisely what Vichy die-hards do not want to face.

If Ophuls is on the side of the Resistance, why then has the reaction of those who fought in it been so embarrassed? Up to mid-1972, France's television (a state monopoly) never showed the film, which had been made for Swiss and West German television companies, and the head of the French television never found the time to see it. Released as a movie, it has reached hundreds of thousands, instead of millions, as it would have on home screens. In this respect, what the mirror reveals about present-day France is doubly fascinating. Gaullist officialdom had two contemporary reasons for resenting Ophuls' work. On the one hand, he and his associates had worked for France's television network (ORTF) until the ''events'' of May 1968. At that time, they took part in the strike which crippled the ORTF and marked a rebellion of many of its employees against government control (especially over news programs). Ophuls and his associates were among those whom the government dismissed once the strike was over. The relative liberalization introduced, after de Gaulle's retirement, by the new Premier, Chaban-Delmas, did not go so far as to endear Ophuls to the management of the ORTF. It did not convince the top bureaucracy of a faction-ridden and politically highly sensitive state enterprise (constantly criticized by vigilant conservative Gaullists for any departure from social orthodoxy and political conformity) to show a movie in which an old French peasant suggests that 80-year old leaders should be thrown to the pigs![3] While two of de Gaulle's wartime supporters and ministers, Mendès-France and d'Astier, speak very highly of de Gaulle, there isn't much else about him in the movie—the short newsreel clipping that shows him reading a speech on the BBC is hardly flattering. Even people less finely attuned to the nuances of anti-Gaullist *contestation* than the bosses of the ORTF could find in the film traces of the "spirit of May". Would this movie have been entirely the same, if it had been made, say, in 1967?

On the other hand, and quite apart from this, the movie challenged what might be called an official myth that had become hallowed with time, and buttressed by a combination of official emphasis and general public silence: not the "myth of the Resistance" (the movie itself shows that it was a noble and formidable reality), but the myth of the French as massively enrolled in or at least standing behind the Resistance, with the exception of a handful of collaborationists and of a small clique of reactionaries. The Official Version makes of France a victorious power, temporarily defeated in an early battle, yet faithful throughout to her cause and her allies, thanks to the Resistance, and fully engaged both in her own liberation and in the defeat of Nazi Germany. The Vichy regime—whose existence so sharply differentiated France's case from that of the other occupied countries whose governments had moved into exile in London—is dismissed as illegal and illegitimate since its creation: a point on which de Gaulle remained intractable, despite the reservations of French courts. How this version developed is easy to understand. The dramas of the war, occupation and liberation eliminated practically the whole of France's political class: the Vichy-ites were purged, most of the political leaders of the Third Republic—whom Vichy had discarded, berated and sometimes jailed or worse—were still held responsible for France's execrable state of unpreparedness in 1939–40, and for the years of internal turmoil and external appeasement in the thirties. The new political class which appeared after the war was of Resistance vintage, whether they belonged to new parties, such

[3]. After various scandals in the ORTF and the resignation of Chaban-Delmas (not unconnected events), a newly appointed and openly political boss of the ORTF has decided both to tighten at once the state's grip on it, in accordance with the Gaullists' demands and—by way of compensation it seems—to show *The Sorrow and the Pity* in the near future.

as the Christian Democrats (MRP), or to old ones, such as the Communists and Socialists. The biggest recruiting asset of the Communist party, after the Liberation, was its heroic role in the Resistance, which it exploited shamelessly, calling itself the party of the "75,000 shot". Jacques Duclos, who was the most important leader of the Party underground, clings to this theme in the movie. There was no major difference between the Fourth and the Gaullist Fifth Republics in this respect, except that a regime headed by General de Gaulle was even less willing to challenge the accepted version, and thanks to its self-assurance and cohesion, even more capable of seeing to it that the official radio and television networks, and constant public ceremonies, remind the French at every occasion of the role of the Resistance and of the Free French, and of the great days of Liberation. De Gaulle's battle for emancipation from American or "Anglo-Saxon" dominance led to an even greater underplaying of the Allies' role in the war. Many of the leaders of the Gaullist party had been war heroes; there was an elite of a few hundred "compagnons de la Libération", distinguished by their deeds in occupied France or in de Gaulle's ranks. Not so paradoxically, the fact that in the early 1970s the Gaullist state was headed by a man, Georges Pompidou, who had not served in the Resistance—he taught in a Paris high school—and the Communist Party by a man, Georges Marchais, who had been drafted by the Laval government to work in Germany for the Nazi war machine and had gone there rather than joining the *maquis*, made it even less likely that the official version would be abandoned by its promoters.

The weight of that version, the persistent, if often submerged division between the two camps of the war years, and most probably the discomfort felt by all those who had lived those years without committing themselves, or had come to feel sorry about their commitment, and who knew the inaccuracies of the Official Version, but feared the squalor of a truer one, all of this resulted in a general unwillingness to dismantle the myth. The only challengers were the surviving Vichyites, whose own casuistry and unrepentent shrillness, denigration of their foes and obstinate arrogance only strengthened the Official Version. In primary and secondary school, little was being said about the war years (partly, of course, because contemporary history is rarely taught). What was said,

xii.

or written in texts, was in conformity with the Official Version. Caught between the regime's celebrations, and the schools' scanty sketches of the myth, surrounded by elders who either preferred not to talk about those painful years or draped themselves in the glory of their exploits, or else marinated in rancor, France's younger generation was growing up in a mixture of indifference, ignorance and exasperation toward these crucial years: they knew little, except that their parents' occasional discussions sounded to them like old veterans' tales of bygone ages.

It is no surprise if the audiences in the movie houses where *The Sorrow and the Pity* is shown are largely composed of young men and women, who have found in this film a way of learning without indoctrination. It is no surprise if officialdom has been less than elated. While the Communists, whose role in the Resistance is stressed in the movie, have not complained, they have not greeted it with enthusiasm: after all, the film punctures the *image d'Epinal* of a nation led by the working class, rising against the oppressors under the guidance of the Communists . . . Gaullist politicians, privately or in interviews, have denounced the movie as an unpatriotic act. History is chaos, so goes their argument, and any selection and interpretation are arbitrary. The official version may not be the total truth, but it has an essence of truth in it, and it has a vital function. To be sure, there were collaborationists, traitors, torturers; a huge majority of the French, after the debacle, had applauded Pétain's determination to take France out of the war and to change the regime. To be sure, many of the people who cheered de Gaulle on the Champs Elysées on that glorious day in August 1944 had come to salute Pétain when he visited the capital four months earlier. But the most important thing for France was to overcome her weaknesses, to play a vital role in the world, to regain her rank and to strengthen her resources, material and moral. This could only be done, not so much by explicitly denying the real shame or "sorrow", as by explicitly emphasizing the equally real heroism and *redressement*. If one wants people to win victories over their very worst flaws, one must appeal to what is noble in them. If one wants to bring out the best in them, it is the best that one must celebrate. Man, said de Gaulle to Malraux, was not made to be guilty, sin is not interesting, the only ethics are those which lead man toward the greater things he carries in himself.[4] If the Official Version had a self-serving function (in that it legitimized and supported the post-war political elite), it had even more of a therapeutic mission.

It is high time that a debate take place about the merits and demerits of this version. Its strengths cannot be dismissed out of hand. France's gravest problem, throughout the thirties and the war years, was a crisis of self-esteem. De Gaulle set himself up as the nurse of France's self-respect. Whatever the failings which the movie exposes—ranging from cowardice for survival to crimes against humanity—they did not compare with those of Nazi Germany: the collaborationists and the murderers were a small minority, the Vichyites grew fewer and fewer as the war went on, popular support for Pétain kept dwindling and turned to a mix of pity, dismay and disgust. There was, therefore, little need to stare at one's evil deeds, to face one's guilt, to purge oneself of lies and sins in order to be sure never to commit them again and to be able to look into the eyes of others. Public contrition was not a precondition of self-respect. In public affairs, moreover, ethics and politics are hard to separate. Denazification was the precondition of the West German march toward status and power, which Adenauer led. In France, on the other hand, any wallowing in shame, any prolonged and extensive purges aimed at weeding out all those who in any way had done wrong, would only have served the designs of those among France's allies who wanted to relegate her to a minor role in the post-war era, and the plans of the Communists at home, who were calling for the most drastic purges and hoped to fill the vacuum. For the last half-century, France's air had been filled with mutual recriminations, charges and counter-charges about who was responsible for decadence and degradation. If other nations had tended to project their troubles on their neighbors, and had to be forced to look at themselves at last, the French had made the mistake of locking themselves into their cage and of tearing themselves apart in it: it was time for them to overcome those demons and to get out of the cage, onto the world stage again. Vichy, in search of a quiet niche in the victorious enemy's domain, had plunged the French into an orgy of breast-beating, which had, as usual, turned

4. Fallen Oaks, *New York, 1972.*

into a lurid spectacle of scapegoat baiting. This was not to be repeated in 1945.

And yet, there were serious flaws in this approach. Official therapeutics and widespread malaise—or justified lack of pride—concerning the national performance in 1940–44 combined in a sort of conspiracy of silence about much that had really happened. It made a genuine assessment of that period far more difficult than for any other troubled and divisive period of French history. Perhaps because it carries no overtones of treason, and even though it is tainted by tortures and massacres, the Algerian war, however recent, can be more easily discussed than the war years. And while aimed at overcoming French weaknesses, the official approach reflects them insofar as it deems the French too immature or too fickle to face themselves without lapsing into either demoralization or chaos; there is a good deal of paternalism here. Moreover, what may have been justified in 1945 is much harder to condone in 1972. Now that the French population consists so largely of boys and girls who were not even born when the war ended, and to whom those distant traumas are hardly different from the turmoils they read about in their history texts, why should not the taboo be lifted? If the revelation of Vichy complicity in Nazi crimes on the one hand, of widespread mediocrity and passivity on the other lifts a veil which the elites and the older generations are eager to keep wrapped around their nakedness, why should the young feel ashamed or guilty? After all, the very "generation gap" protects them from feeling solidarity. The official answer would be, I suspect, that one of Gaullism's assumptions and objectives is precisely the preservation of such solidarity, the duty of each new generation to take on—"*assumer*"—the sum total of French history. The answer would also be that it was highly unfortunate for the challenge of the Official Version to coincide with the May 1968 and post-May challenge of the Gaullist regime. *The Sorrow and the Pity* could not fail to be seen as both an onslaught on the contemporary branches of the Gaullist regime (which pleased the Communists) and a hacking at its historical roots (which worried them).


## II

There was still another reason for the post-war political elites not to be happy about this movie—a reason that has little to do either with May 1968 or with the Official Version. Here we must turn to the second entity mirrored in the movie : war-time France. Some critics of the film did not much mind its having shaken the Gaullist tree, but they thought that it gave a distorted view of France during those years—a myth was in danger of being replaced by a counter-myth. Maybe the very strength and resilience of the myth had invited as mighty and devastating a rebuttal as this one, but two excesses do not make one truth. Maybe the French ought to be obliged to watch this film, on their television screens, in their dining rooms, and forced to face at last the other, seamier side of the story, to compare the indictment with the legend. But isn't there a danger that foreign audiences, especially in nations that have had reasons to resent French post-war actions, or to suspect that the Official Version is a whitewash, will accept only too willingly *The Sorrow and the Pity* as the real and whole truth ?

That it is the "real" truth cannot be questioned. It is easy to use a movie camera for lies—propaganda films sometimes do so brilliantly. But there are no lies here. Marcel Ophuls, in an interview, has stated that his intention had been to show the discrepancy between present testimonies and past reality, the distortions of memory and the soothing role of oblivion for many souls who need to find peace. This he has done superbly—for instance, when he asks Mr. Marius Klein, the shopkeeper, about his old ad denying that he was Jewish; or when he interviews two ancient high school teachers who do not seem capable of bringing their past back to life, or when d'Astier, on the eve of his death, repudiates his earlier demand for drastic purges; or when every German who appears in the film denies responsibility for atrocities or arrests which, invariably, were another service's responsibility. But Ophuls does much more with the passage of time than recording lapses, denials and inconsistencies. He shows how diversely that passage affects different people. He records the bitter and vivid memories of some—the two humane, quietly heroic and so movingly matter-of-fact old peasants, the brothers Grave, who say that their Resistance feats gave them a bad reputation; the successful businessman who used to be Colonel Gaspar in the Resistance, and who now drives a German Mercedes but who remains haunted by the events of these years, upset by the false claims of "the Resistants of the last hour" and contemptuous of those who took no risks then but now lie to themselves. De la Mazière, the former Fascist and French Waffen SS volunteer, is still smarting from Pétain's refusal to see him; as for his revolutionary "past" (he quite perceptively remarks that for the son of a traditional French counter-revolutionary officer to become a Fascist was a form of *contestation*—just as it is today for the son of a Communist to become a *Gauchiste*), it has left him skeptical of ideologies and fearful of commitments. And there is, of course, that unforgettable character out of a Mauriac novel or a Clouzot movie: the hairdresser, Mme. Solange, arrested, tortured and jailed after the Liberation on what she considers to be a trumped-up charge, cooked up by a close friend who imitated her handwriting in an act of vengeance aimed both at her own husband and at Mme. Solange. Whether *her* story is true, we'll never know, but about her own sufferings, and her resentments, and her firm and typical "apolitical" love for Pétain, her hands, her voice, her face, her words allow us no doubts. Also, Ophuls shows men who have not changed at all, and regret nothing: on the one hand, former captain Tausend, still proud of German victories, cheerfully self-righteous and convinced that Alsace is German, or that other ex-soldier of the Third Reich who still resents his capture by the *maquis*; on the other hand, Pierre Mendès-France, as incisive, tough-minded, devoid of illusions or cant, articulate, combative, ironic and proud today as when he was being hounded as a Jew and tried on a fake charge of desertion. If M. Verdier, the pharmacist who is in a way the movie's anti-hero, has changed at all, it is only insofar as he has become a rather opulent bourgeois, as he smugly admits; his feelings haven't.

Truthful when he shows us what time has done to his characters, Ophuls is also right when he tells us what went on in the war years. The thread is provided by two figures. One is the invariably ebullient, bouncy and mindlessly optimistic Maurice Chevalier, singing his silly little patriotic ditties during the phony war, then under Pétain, then after the liberation. He symbolizes both the average guy's resilience and talent for passing through all regimes, and the breezy mediocrity and shallow self-satisfaction that survive all ordeals. (It must be said, however, that there was much more to Chevalier than this; if the use of his songs and dances is a perfectly fair statement of a theme, it is unfair to the man, however much on target insofar as his audiences are concerned). The other figure is M. Verdier, who reveals himself as the perfect *français moyen* of those years: all events are reduced to him—at best, to him and his family. He let, as he put it, the front come to him; the defeat, to him, was like losing a rugby match; eating and prudence were his mottoes—out of fear of starvation he overfed his son born during the occupation. The big event of 1942, for him, was the resumption of hunting. A monster, a scoundrel? Assuredly not. His horizon may be low, his sense of solidarity weak, his display of that form of individualism Tocqueville had prophesied and detested may be annoying, but the other side of the coin is a kind of soft humanity—he had refused to kill a German soldier whom he could have shot, he helped two Jewish girls, his powers of sympathy are genuine enough. But indignation and rebellion are not his forte: the only reaction one could have to the deportations of Jews, he says, was tears—hidden tears: in one's cellar . . . Other characters are revealed as even more mediocre: the hotel keeper at Royat, whose bad memories of the Germans who took over his hotel are limited to the fact that he did not get paid, and to the night when German soldiers tried to bring girls up to their rooms; the bicycle champion who saw no Germans in a city which was not merely occupied, after November 1942, but the scene of violent disturbances. If the movie so often seems a prosecutor's brief, it is not because of the interviewers' questions—the screenplay makes this clearer than the film itself—it is because of the answers they get.

What is, ultimately, frightening about *The Sorrow and the Pity*, is what it reveals to some, and reminds the others, about the climate of quasi-civil war and Nazi occupation. It is Verdier who, characteristically, talks about sorrow and pity: soft feelings again. What seeps from the screen is contempt, hatred and fear. D'Astier, in 1969, explains his bloodthirstiness of 1944 by the fact that throughout the war years he had lived in fear. It is fear which the two high school professors remember, amidst the ruins of their memory, as the main reason why repression and arrests went unchallenged by their colleagues. It is fear which Denis Rake, the British agent who lived in hiding in France, sees as the reason for the bourgeois' caution and cowardice. It is hatred, the kind of hatred that

breeds and feeds civil wars, which, as Mendès-France
reports, inspired the followers of Pétain and Laval
in their campaign against the parliamentarians who
had sailed on the *Massilia* in order to keep fighting,
and in their attacks on the Socialist leader of the
Popular Front, Léon Blum, whom they blamed, ab-
surdly, for France's fall—because the Popular Front
had scared them. It is hatred which that almost
cartoon-like figure, the monarchist resistant Colonel du
Jonchay, still feels toward Communists, and toward
Mendès. It is hatred which bloated Vichy's anti-
Semitism, and the Fascism of young men like de la
Mazière, raised on a diet of antiliberalism, anticom-
munism, and disgust for foreigners and Jews. It is
hatred which led to the Vichy militia's abominations.
It is hatred as well as envy and pettiness disguised
as patriotic duty which turned poison pen letters into
an industry. It is hatred and a passion for hasty
vengeance which swelled the inevitable wave of summary executions in the weeks that preceded and
followed the Liberation. As for contempt, the movie
is steeped in it: the contempt which we, as spectators,
cannot help feeling toward some of the characters on
the screen; the contempt which the former German
occupiers obviously still have for the French who
served them—on the black-market or in bed—or who
came asking for services, such as the right to hold
horse races; the sardonic contempt, barely curbed by
pity and empathy, which old General Spears, Churchill's adviser and de Gaulle's friend turned foe, suggests about a nation that let England down and turns
to military saviors even in defeat; the contempt of
de la Mazière for the glittering nights of occupied
Paris—but also for the drab soldiers of France compared to the healthy torsoes of the Nazis; the contempt
of Mendès (and of his lawyer) for the men who tried
and jailed him. Whoever has not lived through such
a period will get its poisons into his bloodstream,
while watching *The Sorrow and the Pity*.

There is another truth that emerges here, one which
has been mentioned before: a truth about what
cemented each camp. The men of Vichy were those for
whom order was the highest good. War was chaos and a
permanent threat of subversion; only an authoritarian
and reactionary regime could restore and consolidate
"society", undermined by democracy and labor un-
ions and "excessive" freedoms and "foreign" mias-
mas. On the other side were all those for whom

freedom came first, whether it was the lay, republican, humanitarian ideal of freedom the brothers Grave had absorbed in their socialist milieu and in the Republic's public school, or the somewhat less liberal, more narrowly patriotic instinct of freedom from foreign invaders which seems to have animated Colonel Gaspar. That secondary truth—the diversity of each camp—is also brought home by the film. Lamirand, the amiable and gullible engineer who tried in vain to convert French youth to the cult of Pétain, and de la Mazière hardly seem to belong to the same world. D'Astier, the eccentric aristocrat who describes himself as the black sheep of his family, and who, after years of Communist fellow traveling, died a left-wing Gaullist, proclaims—autobiographically—that only "ill-adjusted" people were ripe for the risks of the Resistance; but those admirable brothers Grave, so much in harmony with their hills and their land and their farm, were obviously well adjusted men, who decided that what they had was worth fighting and dying for.

Finally, what is true, even if it hurts, is the portrait of people who, submitted to a barrage of propaganda and later to a deluge of bombs, fearful of famine and reprisals, caught between armies and police forces, uncertain of the future, afraid of the disastrous effects of any commitment, find whatever security is still available only by locking the doors of their homes and hearts, cling to their daily tasks, try to remain unnoticed, and pray for survival. Self-preservation is not the noblest of aims, but it is the most elementary. In the torn country of 1944, with all communications cut, battles raging, rumors on the rampage, executions and ambushes everywhere, each man, each family, each village or town tended to become a little sovereign island again. That this did not prevent an extraordinary revival of community and an explosion of national enthusiasm became clear at the Liberation— about which we see very little, and whose excesses only are mentioned.

Indeed, if nothing here is false, it is not the whole truth which we see. Foreigners should beware of judging war-time France on the basis of this movie alone. *The Sorrow and the Pity* lasts 4½ hours: it is much too short a time for a fair sketch of France in those years. I wish Ophuls could have made a movie twice or three times as long, or a series of movies. Whole chunks of history are missing. The complex, slow way in which public opinion woke up from its escapist dream of archaic reaction and sheltered neutrality, realized that its love affair with Pétain rested on delusions, and gradually recoiled from the harsh realities of oppression and collaboration is not well shown here. There were turning points: Laval's return to power in April 1942, the Allies' invasion of North Africa and Pétain's failure to leave Vichy, in November 1942, the landings in Italy, etc. etc., which are not indicated. The spectator remains under the impression that the parties, salons, theaters and collaborationist movie stars of occupied Paris remained representative of French slackness or corruption throughout the period; this is not at all the case. The Resistance was, of course, not the subject matter of the movie. Even so, it could have been less arbitrarily presented. The movie focuses on Clermont-Ferrand, the capital of Auvergne; but it neither reports the resistance activities of the faculty and students from the University of Strasbourg, in exile in Clermont— which led to massive Nazi repression—nor does it dwell on those of the big Michelin rubber factory, in which management as well as workers took part (one person merely mentions the arrest of Mme. Michelin). While the statement, so often made since 1945 and echoed here by Denis Rake, according to which the "people" and especially the workers joined the Resistance but the bourgeoisie did not, has some truth in it, it is much more true of the industrial and commercial bourgeoisie (with important exceptions, as in Clermont-Ferrand) than of the bourgeoisie of the professions. One would not know it from this film. Not much is said about a group whose impact was enormous, in days when the printed and the spoken word had such a resonance: the intelligentsia. One rather crazy pro-Nazi novelist, Chateaubriand, is shown; why not, on the other side, Malraux or Vercors? More seriously even, the diversity and complexity of French Resistance movements is barely suggested here. Why Duclos, who had little to do with Clermont-Ferrand, appears on the screen is not clear. It was, of course, important that the Communists' skills and sacrifices be evoked; but it would have been equally fair to stress the role of Christian Democrats and priests in the Resistance (the former head of the MRP, Bidault, is interviewed, but talks of other things). Too much emphasis is put on Colonel du Jonchay, who manages to make the Resistance look pretty silly; and while there are moving scenes with ex-Colonel Gaspar, some of the spectators may have felt sorry that the true hero of the movie (along with Mendès), the marvelous old Grave, who knows who was responsible for his deportation but refuses to avenge himself, was a member of the *British* Intelligence Service, not of the *French* Resistance: a small point, perhaps, for foreign audiences today, but a sore one for many Frenchmen, especially at a time when Vichy and the Nazis kept denouncing the rebels as a rabble manipulated by London and Moscow.

Omissions bother me less, however, than what I would call a subtle distortion due to the process of selection. The whole truth is not here, not only because of what is left out altogether, but because of what is emphasized. Of course the Resistance was not a mass movement—less than 250,000 ''membership cards'' were given out by the Veterans' Administration after the war. But would it have been impossible to note how difficult it is to reach even that figure in a largely *petit-bourgeois* country, in which most citizens do have something to lose—beyond their lives and freedoms— if they abandon their daily routine and throw themselves into the adventure of clandestinity? Of course Vichy's anti-Semitic legislation, however autonomous, and Laval's ghastly decisions about the Jews, bitterly recalled by one of his young victims who survived to write eloquently about that sinister episode, Claude Lévy, represent hideous complicity with Nazism at its worst. But to say, as he does, that *France* was the only European country that collaborated, equates the Vichy regime and its police with France, and neglects all the Quislings and Oustachis elsewhere. Moreover, it leaves in the dark all those who helped Jews, foreign or French, to escape and survive. To be sure, Rake and the British pilot downed over France, Evans, pay a tribute to the people who hid them. But—such is the power of the camera—what is said is less deeply convincing than what is shown, and so much of what is shown is grisly or shameful. The Resistance, small as it may have been, would not have had a chance of getting started and organized, and of surviving the highly efficient hounding of the Nazis and of their well-equipped French accomplices, if it hadn't had— especially in 1943–44—the support, active and passive, of millions of Frenchmen, who provided the *maquisards* with false identity papers, food, clothing, shelter and information. Some people—such as de la Mazière—preserved their ''innocence'' and closed their eyes and ears when victims were rounded up and sent to camps and jails. But there were many more who knew, and did their best to save or help these victims. All of this may have been unspectacular; but it was important, in itself and for the record. One does not see much of it here. It is as if the right tune were being sung, but in the wrong key. For Americans, who have never experienced sudden, total defeat and the almost overnight disappearance of their accustomed political elites; who have never lived under foreign occupation; who do not know what Nazi pressure meant; who have never had any apparently legal government, headed by a national hero and claiming total obedience, that sinks deeper and deeper into a morass of impotence, absurdity and crime; who have never had to worry first and last about food and physical survival, the wise and gentle warning of Anthony Eden must be heeded: do not judge too harshly—especially if you keep in mind all that is not graphically recorded here, and if you remember that the movie you watch is both a revelation, and a weapon in a painful domestic battle of the French with their past. . .

## III

*The Sorrow and the Pity* does not only mirror the French of today and those of the war years. Like all works of art, it reflects its author. I have never met Marcel Ophuls, but his movie helps me to know him. He came to France, as a child, when his German parents fled Nazi Germany. Max Ophuls, his father, the famous director of *Liebelei, La Ronde, Lola Montes*, became a French citizen, like many refugees from Central Europe, and served in the French army when the war began. His son, like so many children of aliens, must have been caught in that French melting pot that is almost as effective as, and less publicized than, the American one: France's pot is her school system, her universalistic culture, the seduction of France's intelligence and logic. Then came the catastrophe, and Vichy, its statute of Jews which discriminated against them in various professions—especially the movies—and its vendetta against naturalized refugees. The Ophuls family left for the United States in 1941. They did not return to France until 1950. Max Ophuls, unrecognized in Hollywood, once again found fame in France. Marcel became a movie director too.

This history, I think, explains a great deal. France is Marcel Ophuls' country: how well he knows her ways, her landscapes, the tone of people's conversations, the language of glances and gestures peculiar to her folk, the rhetoric of official propaganda, the atmosphere of her so often stifling provincial towns! But, obviously, his country has deeply hurt him, as a child, in 1940. *The Sorrow and the Pity* is partly an exploration of the wound, partly the cry of a grieving convert—a child in flight from Nazi persecution, who had found new roots in France. As once uprooted people do, he had probably adopted France ever so passionately while she adopted him legally. He had probably fallen in love with the wisdom and poetry of French classics, the turmoil and intensity of French history, the ease and harmony of French daily life, the witty humaneness of the French *peuple*. Marcel Ophuls, growing older, must have found himself increasingly drawn back to these traumatic months of collapse, eerie revolution, sudden reversal of all values, and sudden fear; increasingly, he must have felt the need to come to grips with his own experience, and annoyance with French unwillingness to face the past, with official boastings, with the one-sidedness of the standard—the victors'—history. Both his resentment at the Germans who uprooted him a second time, and his grievances against the French who shattered his love affair, fill the screen. The subtle distortions I have mentioned are not accidental: they tell a story—his own. How do I know this? By listening to the cool, sometimes insinuating, often cutting voice that interviews so many of the characters; and by listening to myself, whose personal history has many points in common with his own, except that I had come to France some years earlier, and not as a refugee, when I was a few months old, and that I remained in France throughout the war as a Frenchified Austrian—French by education and feeling, Austrian only by passport, a partly Jewish alien (my mother not having asked for naturalization in time), in a xenophobic anti-Semitic police state.

Hence both my sympathy and my dissent. The first half of the movie—The Collapse—is almost unassailable: Marcel Ophuls was there, lived through this, and gives us the best account since the first half hour of René Clément's *Forbidden Games*. This was the feeling, of cowardly relief and collective brain concussion, the stunned flight from the war, the terrible blow—incomprehensible then, and, for many, even now—delivered by the British when they attacked the French fleet at Mers-el-Kébir, the search for peace and quiet and discipline—and scapegoats—under the grand old oak, Marshal Pétain, the clarion calls for atonement, the arrogant wails of self-flagellation, and the daily miseries of partial occupation and food shortages. But Marcel Ophuls was not there later on: hence the weaknesses of the second half, The Choice. He was not there, when the "armies of the shadows" gathered in the woods, when resistance networks defied the Gestapo and the Vichy militia and dropped their coded messages in the cities' mailboxes, when the morale of an exhausted and restless nation was suspended on the exhortations of a handful of spokesmen at the BBC and on the eloquence of writers whose real names were disguised at the bottom of ill-printed columns in clandestine newspapers and confidential pamphlets. These were the days of hope and fervor, when even those who were not heroic began to live vicariously with the heroes, in an atmosphere of passionate anticipation that makes anything in the post-war world seem drab or drained by comparison. This is where the Official Version is vindicated: the grand Gaullist metaphor of a nation that overcomes its initial weakness, daunts its demons, climbs the slope again, and makes the final victory partly its own, surely flatters the French too much by downplaying the doubts and divagations of the earlier period, or the opportunism and savagery that marred the climb. But it is, basically, not false. Who did not live, in a French town or village, the weeks just before and after the Liberation, does not know the bliss of being alive at the end of an unspeakable ordeal, or the bliss of being happy with and proud of those amidst whom one had come through. Much of what went on earlier can be forgiven—the little capitulations and the small acts of selfishness and meanness, if not the cruelties and calls for murder—because of the price paid, and of the slowly opening eyes, and of the *revanche* that was also a redemption, later on. If Maurice Chevalier tells one part of the story—the part I also remember so well, from the miserable radio of 1939 or 1941—surely Jean Moulin, the martyred leader of the Resistance, and Charles de Gaulle's inflexible genius tell the other part. Both parts are true; but since we all judge—maybe we shouldn't, but we can't help it—my own verdict is not at all as severe as Marcel Ophuls'. On the scales of history, when it will at last be possible to weigh men, their acts, and their effects more fairly, the great things will be weightier than the mean ones. In Marcel Ophuls' movie, Verdier and the two almost senile schoolteachers remain a nagging, almost deafening counterpoint to the Graves, to Gaspar and to Mendès. In my memory, the schoolteacher—now 74, and still vibrant—who taught me French history, gave me hope in the worst days, dried my tears when my best friend was deported along with his mother, and gave false papers to my mother and me so that we could flee a Gestapo-infested city in which the complicity of friends and neighbors was no longer a sufficient guarantee, this man wipes out all the bad moments, and the humiliations, and the terrors. He and his gentle wife were not Resistance heroes, but if there is an average Frenchman, it was this man who was representative of his nation; and for that, France and the French will always deserve our tribute, and have my love.

—*Stanley Hoffmann*

The Guignol welcomes Hitler and Goering.

GEORGES BIDAULT, (1899- )
Bidault was emprisoned by the Germans from 1941 to 1943. Upon release he joined the "Combat" wing of the Resistance movement and published the *Bulletin de la France combattante.* After Jean Moulin was arrested in 1943, Bidault became president of the "Conseil national de la Résistance" (CNR), the group created by Moulin to coordinate Resistance movements in both zones of France. After the war, Bidault became Secretary of Foreign Affairs and served as Prime Minister from 1949 to 1950. His strong opposition to de Gaulle's stance in favor of Algerian independence led him to exile in Brazil. After a general amnesty was declared for opponents of Algerian independence in 1967, he returned to France where he is now living.

MATHEUS BLEIBINGER
A mason from Bavaria. Bleibinger was taken prisoner by the Auvergne maquis in Clermont-Ferrand at the time of the Liberation.

CHARLES BRAUN
Restaurant owner in Clermont-Ferrand.

MAURICE BUCKMASTER
Retired British colonel. Former director of the British espionage network (S.O.E.).

PIERRE LE CALVEZ
Movie theater owner in Clermont-Ferrand. After German troops occupied the southern zone of France in November, 1942, le Calvez's movie theater was renamed a "Soldatenkino," a theater showing movies for German soldiers.

COMTE RENE DE CHAMBRUN
Chambrun is the son-in-law of Pierre Laval. For twenty years he has been trying to rehabilitate Laval's reputation and clear his name from accusations of treason. The enormous file gathered by him and his wife was published in France in three volumes by Plon, and published in the U.S. by The Hoover Institute.

EMILE COULAUDON

Formerly called "Colonel Gaspar" while serving as the head of the Auvergne maquis group of the Resistance, Coulaudon now works for the Philips Company in Clermont-Ferrand.

MESSIEURS DANTON and DIONNET

Monsieur Danton is a teacher at the Lycée Pascal in Clermont-Ferrand. Monsieur Dionnet is a librarian at the same school.

JACQUES DUCLOS, (1896- )

During the First World War, Duclos was wounded and taken prisoner by the Germans. After the war he joined the Communist Party and was elected to the Chamber of Deputies in 1926. He served until 1932, and was re-elected in 1935. In 1958 he was elected to the Senate. He played an important part in the Popular Front alliances prior to the outbreak of World War II, and during the war he became the head of the clandestine Communist Party of France. He is the editor of various newspapers and regularly writes editorials for the Communist daily *l'Humanité*.

ROBERT ANTHONY EDEN,
FIRST EARL OF AVON,
(1897-   )
Anthony Eden served as
Great Britain's Secretary of
State for Foreign Affairs
from 1935 to 1938, and as
Secretary of War during
1940. From 1940 to 1945 he
was once again Secretary
for Foreign Affairs, and
from 1942 to 1945, leader of
the House of Commons as
well. He became Prime
Minister of Great Britain in
1955 and remained in that
office until 1957. He published his memoirs, *Full
Circle,* in 1960.

FLIGHT SERGEANT EVANS
Retired British pilot, shot
down in Auvergne while flying an RAF mission in May,
1944.

MARCEL FOUCHE-DEGLIAME
Former leader in the "Combat" wing of the Resistance
movement, and editor of
their newspaper of the same
name. The "Combat" group
consisted mostly of French
officers and Christian Democrats.

RAPHAEL GEMINIANI
Champion professional cyclist from Clermont-Ferrand.

ALEXIS GRAVE
Farmer in Yronde, a hamlet near Clermont-Ferrand. He is the brother of Louis Grave.

LOUIS GRAVE
Brother of Alexis Grave, also a farmer in Yronde.

COLONEL R. DU JONCHAY
A retired French colonel formerly active in the Resistance; an anticommunist with Catholic monarchist leanings.

MARIUS KLEIN
Shopkeeper in Clermont-Ferrand.

GEORGES LAMIRAND

Lamirand served as Minister of Youth from 1941 to 1943 under the Vichy government. He is now mayor of La Bourboule, a small town near Clermont-Ferrand.

MONSIEUR LEIRIS

Former mayor of Combronde, a small town near Clermont-Ferrand; Resistance fighter in the Auvergne maquis.

DR. CLAUDE LEVY

A writer and biologist once active in the "Franc-Tireur" group within the Resistance movement. He has written the most complete account of Jewish persecution in France during the Occupation.

CHRISTIAN DE LA MAZIERE

The son of an aristocratic family, a youthful supporter of the extreme right-wing in 1940, de la Mazière served during the war as a volunteer for the "Charlemagne" company, the French division of the Waffen S.S. who fought with the Germans on the Eastern Front. In 1972 he published his memoirs of the period, *Reveur casqué*.

PIERRE MENDES-FRANCE,
(1907-   )

A lawyer, Mendès-France served as a deputy from the department of Eure in Normandy from 1932 to 1939. In 1934 he was elected Mayor of Louviers, a town in Normandy. In the 1936 Popular Front government of Léon Blum, he was named Undersecretary of State for Finance. In 1938 he flew on missions to Syria. As a consequence of the Massilia affair, he was arrested in Morocco in August, 1940, and taken to jail in Clermont-Ferrand in October, where he was convicted of desertion and sentenced to six years in prison. Two years later he escaped to London, where he joined the Lorraine unit of the RAF and flew numerous missions over France. Immediately after the Liberation, de Gaulle named Mendès-France his Secretary of Finance. He served again in the Chamber of Deputies from 1946 to 1955 and, as Prime Minister from 1954 to '55, he successfully negotiated an end to the war in Indochina. His memoirs of his trial and imprisonment, *Liberté, liberté chérie,* were published by Didier in New York in 1943.

COMMANDANT MENUT
French army officer from Clermont-Ferrand, formerly active in the Resistance movement.

**DR. ELMAR MICHEL**
Chairman of the Board of Salamander Shoes, Inc., a major West German shoe manufacturer also active in France and England. During the occupation, Michel served as general economic advisor to the German Military Command in France.

**MONSIEUR MIOCHE**
Owner of hotel in Royat, a village on the outskirts of Clermont-Ferrand. The hotel was used during the occupation to house German forces.

**DENIS RAKE**
Denis Rake served inside occupied France as an intelligence agent for the S.O.E., the British espionage network.

**MAITRE HENRI ROCHAT**
A lawyer from Clermont-Ferrand, Rochat defended Pierre Mendès-France in his trial for desertion in Clermont-Ferrand at the end of 1940.

DR. PAUL SCHMIDT
Chief interpreter for Adolf
Hitler from 1934 to 1944.

MADAME SOLANGE
Hairdresser from Château-
gué, a little village outside
Clermont-Ferrand.

MAJOR GENERAL SIR EDWARD
SPEARS, (1886-    ).
Spears became the British
Prime Minister's personal
representative to the French
Minister of Defense in May
1940. A month later, after
the German–French armi-
stice, he was appointed head
of the British mission to
General de Gaulle. During
the war he conducted mis-
sions to Syria and Lebanon.
His book concerning Pétain
and de Gaulle, *Two Men
Who Saved France,* was
published in 1966.

HELMUT TAUSEND
Former Wehrmacht captain stationed in Clermont-Ferrand from 1942 to 1944.

ROGER TOUNZE
Editor for *La Montagne,* a newspaper in Clermont-Ferrand.

MARCEL VERDIER
Pharmacist in Clermont-Ferrand.

EMMANUEL D'ASTIER DE LA VIGERIE, (1900-1969)
Emmanuel d'Astier de la Vigerie, a navy officer who joined the Resistance after the collapse in 1940, created the "Mouvement Libération Sud," one of the most important Resistance organizations in Vichy France. In 1942 he was sent to London, and afterwards to Algiers. After the Liberation, he was appointed Secretary of Interior by de Gaulle and he

published the daily newspaper *Libération*. He later became president of the World Council for Peace and was named Chevalier de la Légion d'Honneur. He died in 1969.

GENERAL WALTER WARLIMONT, (1895-    )
During the First World War, Warlimont served as Battery Commander for the German forces in the West and in Italy. In 1929 he was attached to the U.S. Army for one year to study industrial mobilization. In the summer of 1939 he was appointed military ambassador of the Third Reich's War Minister to General Franco in Spain. In 1938 he was named chief of the National Defense section of the Supreme Command of the Wehrmacht. He was subsequently promoted to lieutenant general. In September of 1944 he was transferred to the OKH Command pool. In 1962 he wrote *Inside Hitler's Headquarters 1939-45,* which was published in the U.S. in 1964.

Norddeutscher Rundfunk, Télévision Rencontre, and Télévision Suisse Romande present:

# THE SORROW AND THE PITY

Chronicle of a French City under the German Occupation

A Film by Marcel Ophuls

**PART I: THE COLLAPSE**
**PART II: THE CHOICE**

Director:
Marcel Ophuls

Photography:
André Gazut
Jurgen Thieme

Editing:
Claude Vadja

Editing Assistants:
Heidi Endruwelt
Wiebke Vogler

Assistant Cameraman:
Alain Demartines

Screenplay & Interviews:
Marcel Ophuls
André Harris

Sound:
Bernard Migy

Mixing:
Wolfgang Schroeter

Music:
the voice of
Maurice Chevalier

Production:
André Harris
Alain de Sedouy
(TV-Rencontre)

Production Director:
Wolfgang Theile

Assistant Director:
Claude Vadja

Documentarists:
Eliane Filippi
(France)
Christoph Derschau
(Germany)
Suzy Benhiat
(Great Britain)

## A WEDDING IN GERMANY, MAY 1969

HELMUT TAUSEND, Captain of the Wehrmacht in
Clermont:
My dear children, your stomachs are full, but I think
you will still be able to listen to a few words. Thirty
years ago your mother and I were married, and
although the sky was still blue then, there were dark
clouds gathering over the horizon—the clouds of
the Second World War. All of us here today
wholeheartedly wish you will be spared those
hardships.

### CLERMONT-FERRAND, APRIL 1969

Clermont-Ferrand, 134,000 inhabitants, is the principal town
of the department of Puy de Dôme and the capital of the

**Clermont-Ferrand.**

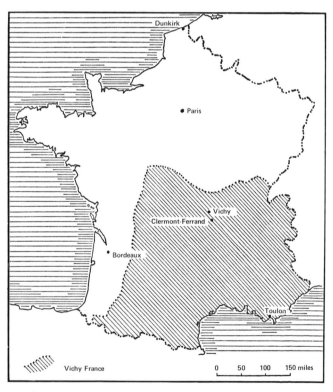

Dunkirk

Paris

Vichy

Clermont-Ferrand

Bordeaux

Toulon

Vichy France

0    50    100    150 miles

province of Auvergne. It is 387 kilometers from Paris, and
59 kilometers from Vichy. Vichy—which was France's
capital from 1940 to 1944.

Nearby lies Gergovie, the Gallic city which was
Vercingetorix's fortress and the place where he was
defeated by Julius Caesar.

••••••••••••••••••••••••••••••••••••••••••••••••••••••••••••••••••••••••••••••••••••••••••••

A father speaks to his children of a more recent defeat—

MARCEL VERDIER, pharmacist in Clermont:
In '39 I was twenty seven years old. Being the father
of a large family, I wasn't sent to the Front—the
Front being the Maginot line, right? I was sent to
Montferrand, on the outskirts of Clermont, and that
is when our milkman's wife, Madame Michel,
reproached me for not having gone to the Front.
After the defeat of the country, I told her: "It was
pointless for me to go to the Front because the Front
came to me."

DAUGHTER OF MARCEL VERDIER:
In the Resistance Movement, was there anything else
besides courage?

MARCEL VERDIER:
Well, there certainly was that. But personally what
I felt most often in those years was a sense of sorrow
and pity.

The Verdier family at home.

| | |
|---|---|
| Le Colonel était d'Action Française, | The colonel was a right winger |
| Le Commandant était un modéré, | The major was a moderate |
| Le Capitaine était pour le diocèse, | The captain loved the Church |
| Et le Lieutenant boulottait du curé. | The lieutenant hated the clergy |
| Le Juteux, était un fervent extrèmiste, | The sergeant major was a wild extremist |
| Le Sergent un socialiste convaincu, | The sergeant was a dedicated socialist |
| Le Caporal inscrit sur toutes les listes, | The corporal bet on everyone and everything |
| Et le deuxième classe au PMU. | The buck private bet on horses only. |
| Et tout ça, ça fait D'excellents Francais, D'excellents soldats, | Yet they all march in step |
| Qui marchent au pas | And they are all terrific Frenchmen |
| En pensant que la République, | And they are all terrific soldiers |
| C'est encore le meilleur régime ici bas, | And they say their Republic's |
| Et tous ces gaillards, qui pour la plupart, | The best thing going |
| Ne sont pas du même avis en politique, | And they all agree on wanting just one thing: |
| Les v'la tous d'accord, Quel que soit leur sort, Ils désirent tous désormais | To be left alone, once and for all. |
| Qu'on leur foute une bonne fois la paix! | |

# The Sorrow and the Pity

Chronicle of a French city under the German occupation.
First Part: The Collapse

Two brothers, farmers of Auvergne, live near Clermont-Ferrand. The German occupation has left them much to remember.

Is that your village out there?

6.

LOUIS GRAVE, farmer near Clermont:
Yes. I was born there. I was born next door to the
church and later we lived in the farm opposite the
school. No matter what, you always love your village.

**When you were at Buchenwald, did you often think about
it?**

LOUIS GRAVE
Not much.

The brothers Grave at their farm.

**Not about your village?**

LOUIS GRAVE:
No. Some of us did, but you didn't really think about
anything, except saving your skin, and that's all.
I speak for myself alone; that is my own point of
view. There were some who cried. I saw them crying
and I would say to myself: Well this one will not
come out of this. . . You couldn't do that. You had
to think about yourself first, and later about the
others, afterwards. . . .

7.

**This politician, too, has reasons to remember.**

PIERRE MENDES-FRANCE, former Prime Minister of
France:
It was for me an unforgettable experience. Perhaps
in the long run I may feel differently, but I don't
think it has affected either my opinions or my
behavior.

**Hasn't it left you somewhat bitter towards French people?**

PIERRE MENDES-FRANCE:
No. It showed me that when certain tendencies,
certain prejudices are whipped up, when they are
stimulated and fed, they come back to life, and that
you must always be on guard, that young people
must be prepared against this type of propaganda,
that we must talk to them, perhaps more than we did
one or two generations ago.

**The director of the Philips Company in Clermont also has
reason to remember.**

EMILE COULAUDON, called GASPAR, former leader of
the Auvergne Maquis:
I think that... going into a restaurant where four
Germans are seated and being told: ''There are no
steaks left—the four last ones are for those gentlemen
there, there aren't any for you.'' That in itself was a
small frustration, although it was a real one since
the steak came from our Auvergne cattle, and we
certainly should have the right to eat it before giving
it to foreigners. That's the first point, simple enough
but true. Second, there was the curfew which told us:
''Tonight you want to go out. Well, you can't. You've
got to be in bed by seven tonight.'' We were under
surveillance. We were in a Nazi, in a totalitarian
regime—call it Nazi or whatever you want—and it's
worth fighting, it's even worth dying, rather than live
in slavery. . . . And that's why we resisted.

LOUIS GRAVE, farmer near Clermont:
They ought to think about making a lasting peace,
because there's nothing more silly than fighting.

8.

That's what I think myself. And, well, it depends on why you are fighting.

**Do you think those who fight always know why?**

LOUIS GRAVE:
I don't believe so; some fanatics, a few know why maybe.

**But you knew, didn't you?**

LOUIS GRAVE:
Oh yes. I knew.

**Yet you are not a fanatic.**

LOUIS GRAVE:
No. But when I went to war in '40—I left in '39 on September the 2nd—I was sent to Modane. Well, what was I supposed to do? I didn't know anything. I was going to kill people I had never seen, you must understand. People who had probably done me no harm. Afterwards of course, when they came to France, they gave us a good beating. . . .

FRENCH NEWSREEL, *On the Maginot Line:*
*Our soldiers are enjoying a rest, but they remain ready to fight. When facing the enemy they display all the qualities of victors: patience, courage, vigilance, resolution, confidence. . . .*

PIERRE MENDES-FRANCE, former Prime Minister of France:
In well-intentioned circles, in social circles in Paris, people sympathized with the misfortunes of our soldiers, misfortunes which were nothing compared with what was to come later. . . alas. And so, during this period, these kind hearts tried to relieve the boredom of our soldiers. Obviously, there must have been some pretty boring days for the soldiers in the bunkers of the Maginot Line. So some well-intentioned ladies of the Parisian bourgeoisie organized a committee to entertain our valiant soldiers. And to provide them with a more pleasant landscape. Their idea was to plant rose bushes along the Maginot Line, so that it would be prettier, cosier . . . more attractive. And so people subscribed, sent along their checks, all for planting rose bushes to

Radio report from the Front.

Life inside the Maginot line. This fortification was built in 1930.

10.

hide those inhuman, ugly cement walls from our soldiers, to give them. . . to let them live in a more agreeable. . . to keep them from thinking about the misfortunes hanging over their heads and the horrors which were to come later. . . .

GERMAN NEWSREEL, *May 10, 1940:*
*The infantry, deployed in all directions, marches onwards. In Oisemont, a tank sets the giant distillery into flame.*

HELMUT TAUSEND, Captain of the Wehrmacht in Clermont:
In Poland it was all over in fifteen days, and in France we thought it would go pretty fast too, because we all wanted to get back to our families again. Well, that's exactly what happened: France was finished within a month.

LOUIS GRAVE, farmer near Clermont:
Of course there were many attacks, but the heaviest was at Oing, on the Belgian frontier. The Belgian blockhouses were not finished, but we had to take up our defensive positions in them anyway.

ALEXIS GRAVE, farmer near Clermont:
The Germans appeared in front of us with tanks and armored cars. As for us, all we had was machine guns

1940: **German troops marching down the Champs Elysées.**

and automatic rifles. The Germans destroyed everybody inside all at once, since we were such a beautiful target. There were no firing slits, there was nothing. The armor-plated doors weren't even hung yet. Listen, we did. . . we fell back, we must have gone at least thirty kilometers. We saw no troops, none at all, not a single one. . . No troops, nothing. Nothing at all.

GENERAL WALTER WARLIMONT, former aide to Supreme Command of the Wehrmacht:
First of all I'd like to stress the fact that at least at German headquarters, nobody expected such a quick and total victory. We soldiers, unlike Hitler, were convinced that we would find the same opponent as in the First World War—a determined, courageous adversary, ready to fight to the end. And in this respect, unfortunately, Hitler was right: he never tired of repeating that the French would be unable to pick up again their performance of the First World War. . . and he never missed the chance, when he made this prophecy, of adding some derogatory and contemptuous comment on the moral and psychological state of France in general.

GERMAN NEWSREEL, *1940:*
*In the vicinity of Noyon, with his advance guard driving forward into enemy territory, Field Marshal Stumme and his aides take many "unexpected" prisoners. . . .*

*At first there are just a few, but then more and more keep coming. And among these prisoners, the mixed rabble of the armies of all nations: carriers of the civilization of "la grande nation." In truth, a cultural shame for the white race.*

*These then are the black brothers of the French* poilu.
    [shots of African soldiers.]

*Just a few days ago Chamberlain explained to an American that England with her Allies was leading the guardians of civilization against medieval barbarity.*

*These then are the "guardians of civilization"* . . .
    [shots of African soldiers.]
*and these are the "barbarians."*
    [German soldiers marching in step.]

12.

*This is the war of the French and English plutocrats,
a war they have lighthandedly launched without
even considering the consequences of their trickery,
a war on behalf of the English Lords which they
will fight not only to the last* poilu, *but down to the
last house left on the French homeland.*

---

GERMAN NEWSREEL, *1940:*
*These cars have run out of gas for good.*

*The Jewish warmongers and Parisian plutocrats had
wanted to take their trunks full of gold and precious
stones and escape with them in these automobiles,
but they did not get far. Soon their tanks were
empty. Roads were hopelessly jammed, so these
England-worshipping deserters and traitors of the
people then tried to escape on foot with their
fortune.*

*And here are the people of France who were
heedlessly evacuated and then caught up by the flood
of fleeing French troops. Now at last these people
can return to their towns and villages.*

*The German peoples are spared all this misery. For
this we must thank the Führer and his soldiers.*

June 6, 1940: Parisian refugees fleeing capital.

June 15, 1940: last refugees leave Paris.

Refugees and tanks pass each other along road.

14.

PIERRE MENDES-FRANCE, former Prime Minister of France:
In those days, there was this tremendous groundswell of panicstricken, frightened people. . . . As it happened, I was on leave at the end of April, so I was in Paris at the beginning of May when the German offensive began. On the roads people were losing their heads, panicked by the bombardments, taking along with them what little they had been able to gather: kids, cats, valuables. Some of them had carts, some were on bicycles. It was a strange and dreadful sight. And it was all the more frightening since the Germans did not hesitate to bomb or machine gun these columns of refugees in order to block the roads and make them useless for our soldiers, so that—and I saw this—you would find here or there corpses of men, women, horses, shells of automobiles, in effect a real vision of hell. . . and always this stream, this flood of people heading for the South. . . .

HELMUT TAUSEND, Captain of the Wehrmacht in Clermont:
What did we feel? What did we see? We saw destroyed villages, burnt soil. It was rather a shaking sight, I must say.

**People on the road?**

HELMUT TAUSEND:
Yes, they were running away from us, "the wicked enemy."

**Why do you say "wicked"? You were not wicked?**

HELMUT TAUSEND:
Well, in the beginning we were considered "the enemy," ready to bathe the whole country in fire and blood; but then people soon realized we meant no harm and so they quickly became reassured.

PIERRE MENDES-FRANCE:
The officers, the general staff, had obviously lost their footing. The breakdown of railways and of the road network, the breakdown of communications, created a situation where the plans that military people may have conceived were suddenly shattered and useless.

15.

Besides, there was in certain military circles a state of mind which could also be found among certain civilians : they entered the war without enthusiasm. After all, they were living in a. . . I do not say they were traitors—there were very few traitors the way I see it—but still the attitude ''better Hitler than Léon Blum'' had done a great deal of damage in bourgeois circles. . . and those were the circles that many military men belonged to.

**June 14th, 1940. The Germans occupy Paris. In Clermont, as well as all over the country, people fight one another for news. The local paper of Clermont, Le Moniteur, calls upon its readers to keep up the fighting, to struggle valiantly, to hold on, to stay free. Who is the owner of this anti-defeatist newspaper? Pierre Laval, Auvergne politician, who at the same time is preparing France's surrender in Bordeaux.**

**The last government of the Third Republic is retreating to the South step by step. Paul Reynaud wants to continue the fight, but already Philippe Petain, a new member of the cabinet, is peeping over his shoulder. At Briare, Winston Churchill and Anthony Eden meet their Allies for the last time.**

**At left: Pétain and Reynaud.**

ANTHONY EDEN, former Prime Minister of Great Britain:
My impression was always that Reynaud wanted to

go on with the fight, that he was absolutely firm and calm. The position would have been difficult for whoever occupied it. Yes. Besides, I had the impression—in fact he told Churchill and me—that he was not very pleased to have Pétain imposed on his government.

**Did he already foresee. . . ?**

Anthony Eden in 1969.

ANTHONY EDEN :
He could already foresee difficulties. As for myself —when I was a young man I had been a soldier in the First World War, and for me Pétain was the hero of Verdun. He had changed with age, what can you expect ? I am quite convinced he thought he was protecting the cities of France ; in fact, during dinner he spoke about it. He said : "It is awful to see the destruction of some of our most beautiful cities." And I had to answer to him : "I quite agree with you but," and this is a difficult thing to say for an Englishman, "there are worse things than the destruction of cities." But I could see he was not convinced. The next day, which happened to be my birthday, Churchill and I flew over in separate

17.

planes. We were flying very low. It was in June. Nothing is more beautiful than the Normandy countryside, or the Brittany coast. And I kept saying: Shall I ever see it again? And it did not seem too likely at the time.

London during the war: Anthony Eden, with gas mask, on his way to meet Chamberlain.

PIERRE MENDES-FRANCE:

Yes. But there was suddenly a sort of metamorphosis

in the political scene and the atmosphere in
Bordeaux was abominable. Treason was spreading
openly—the need to surrender, the desire to come
to an understanding with the winners at any price.
Anglophobia, which is traditional in France,
surfaced quickly. All this was flaunted with a sort
of dreadful cynicism. No one mentioned the
misjudgments of the military chiefs. No, instead
all the mistakes were attributed to Léon Blum, to the
Popular Front, etc., etc. And then many people
accepted the country's misfortunes and consoled
themselves by seeking revenge in internal politics
. . . and, as you know, this tendency could only
increase as things developed.

**June 16th. The French government sits in Bordeaux. Paul
Reynaud is outvoted by the members of his government
who refuse to leave metropolitan France. Pétain becomes
head of the government.**

GERMAN NEWSREEL:
*The Adolf Hitler S.S. Division enters Vichy*

MARCEL VERDIER, pharmacist in Clermont:
I had a very humiliating experience. I was sent off
on a mission on an English motor bike. I headed out
for Paris and met some columns coming the other
way, and since I am a rather absent-minded person,
I thought that they were running away and that
some English troops were running after them. Then,
with them going one way and me the other way, I
realized they were wearing swastikas on their helmets
and I thought: "I better not go any further." But
no one asked me anything. Everyone was going about
his business, me going my way and they going theirs.
And so I just went back home.

**But the battle, what there is of a battle, still goes on. The
Adolf Hitler S.S. Division takes over Clermont-Ferrand.
For three days the German troops occupy the city. Zepp
Dietrich, the commanding officer, plays the victor on the
place Jaude, while his crack regiment shine their boots
in front of the baffled population before moving on to new
victories. The Germans will not return to Clermont until
November, 1942.**

GERMAN NEWSREEL:
*In Saint-Etienne, near Clermont, a whole infantry*

*regiment hands over its arms without a fight.*

- - - - - - - - - - - - - - - - - - - - - - - - - - - - - - - - - - - - - - -

ROGER TOUNZE, newspaperman in Clermont:
Well at the beginning I did not understand anything,
just like everybody else. On June 24th, in the
morning, the lieutenant gave a beautiful speech, and
then Marshal Pétain, the only marshal we had, sued
for an armistice. I knew what an armistice was, but
I did not fully realize what a marshal was.

MARCEL VERDIER, pharmacist in Clermont:
I never felt extremely attracted to the Pétain regime,
but even so, like all the other forty million
Frenchmen who lived through that period and
through that particular day when I saw our army
routed, when I saw that the Germans were in
Biarritz and that the whole of France was invaded,
and that nothing was to be done about it, well I
felt as all the others did: there must be someone
who can stop this massacre.

FRENCH NEWSREEL, *Pétain addresses the nation in a
radio speech:*
*My fellow Frenchmen, at the request of the President
of the Republic, I assume from today the leadership
of the French government. Sure of the loyalty of our
admirable army, which is fighting with a heroism
worthy of a long military tradition against an enemy
superior in number and in arms, sure that its
magnificent resistance has fulfilled our duties to our
allies, sure of the support of veterans whom I have
had the privilege to lead, sure of the confidence of
the whole of the people, I make to France the gift
of my person, to mitigate her misfortune. In these
painful hours, I think of the poor, destitute refugees
walking along our roads. I offer them my compassion
and my solicitude. It is with a heavy heart that I
tell you today: we must stop fighting. Last night I
approached the adversary to ask if he were willing
to seek with me, soldier to soldier, after the battle
and in good faith, a means of ending the hostilities.*

GERMAN NEWSREEL, *loudspeaker carries news of
Pétain's speech to German soldiers:*
*From Supreme Command Headquarters an
announcement of historical importance: The Prime
Minister of the newly-formed French government,*

**Album cover for the recorded speeches of Marshal Pétain.**

*Marshal Pétain, explained in a radio speech to the
people of France that their country must
immediately lay down its arms.*

> [German troops sing:]
> *Forwards! Forwards!*
>    *Forwards!*
> *Forwards soldiers!*
> *Over the Meuse, the Scheldt*
>    *and the Rhine!*
> *We are marching*
>    *victoriously*
> *Into France!*

MADAME TAUSEND, wife of Helmut Tausend:
Of course I was happy about the victory.

MARCEL VERDIER, Pharmacist in Clermont:
I felt about the defeat a little the way I felt losing
rugby matches when I used to play that game. I
don't like losing sixty to nothing, and I don't like
losing right away.

GERMAN NEWSREEL, *French WWI monument:*
*The memorial which was to perpetuate the memory*
*of Germany's submission in November, 1918....*

The signing of the armistice at Rethondes.

Is it true that France had promised England not to conclude a separate armistice?

ANTHONY EDEN, former Prime Minister of Great
Britain:
Well, I believe—this was before I was in the
government—I think we agreed that neither one
nor the other would stop the fighting. I believe that's
right.

Without the other's consent?

ANTHONY EDEN:
Without the other's consent. But we did not speak
about this at all when Churchill and I were there,
because we accepted France's position. He said, at
Briare, that he accepted it.

Did he say he accepted an armistice?

ANTHONY EDEN:
No, but he said: "We accept the possibility that you
cannot go on. We accept it. . . ," without speaking of
an armistice.

Yes, but there is a huge difference between a cease-fire and
an armistice.

ANTHONY EDEN:
Yes. So he simply said: "We realize that you cannot
go on." We understood this clearly. It was obvious.
Then the question was "What are you going to do?"
I even sent Churchill a little note after our return
from Briare—I believe it has been published since
then—saying simply that we had to maintain this
distinction: if France cannot go on with the fighting,
that is one thing; but if she ever collaborates with
the enemy, that is something else.

---

GERMAN NEWSREEL:
*La Madeleine. The Führer marches into Paris by
surprise in the early hours of the morning. He also
visits these other sites: Place de la Concorde, the Arc
de Triomphe, Trocadéro. A view of the Eiffel Tower.
At the left of the Führer, Professor Speer.*

June 15, 1940: Hitler visits Paris.

MONSIEUR LEIRIS, former Mayor of Combronde,
resister:
Let me tell you that when the armistice came there
were quite a few Frenchmen, quite a few who did
not want to go on with the war, who said, "Oh well,
that's that." Marshal Pétain kept his head about
him down there in Vichy. I was there! In every
district and in every parish he formed what they
called the "French Legion."

**The Legion of. . .**

MONSIEUR LEIRIS:
The Legion of Veterans of the First World War.
Every Sunday they went, except me—I was the only
one that never set foot there. They went to raise the
colors in the marketplace over there, every Sunday
morning, with the sickle and the hammer, the sickle
and. . . not the sickle, the sword. The francisque, the
sword. . . no, that's not it. And they were all given
a beret. A beret! Of course, I myself never ever
set foot there, not on your life. When I saw all that,
I understood right away what it was all about.

24.

**And this old marshal proposing an armistice in honor, etc.—as a young Frenchman, how did you feel about this justification of defeat? Didn't it shock you?**

CHRISTIAN DE LA MAZIERE, former volunteer in the French Waffen S.S.:
Of course not, since it was precisely the fatal consequence of a certain policy. . . . And those were going to be the themes of the Vichy government's propaganda: if we have been defeated, then the fault lies with the political parties which have torn the country apart over the years.

**How did that catch-phrase go: ''Those parties which have done us so much harm.'' I can't remember which was the. . . It was. . .**

CHRISTIAN DE LA MAZIERE
Oh no, there was this business of ''the lies. . .''
''I hate the lies which have done us so much harm,'' that's it.

**And also at this time came the famous call for resistance from that other man—General de Gaulle—which very few Frenchmen actually heard. Making this film we have yet to meet someone who did hear it.**

CHRISTIAN DE LA MAZIERE:
Well as far as I'm concerned, I never heard it.

**You were a pilot. I suppose there must have been some people in your units who chose to ''continue the struggle'' as we used to say then. Were you tempted at all?**

CHRISTIAN DE LA MAZIERE:
There were not so many at the time. . . we really ought to get the facts straight. There was a majority who tried to reach North Africa before the Armistice, that is true. But then things calmed down. And anyway there were not very many of them.

**Did it cross your mind?**

CHRISTIAN DE LA MAZIERE:
Yes, of course. But not for long. My father made it quite clear to me that Marshal Pétain would guarantee the coming of a new order.

**And so the victor of Verdun guarantees the honor of**

France and the new order—of which he himself is the incarnation. This policy seems to be not only desirable but also necessary to many of his countrymen. They give their confidence as well as their respect to the Marshal. In Clermont the spirit of renewal flows through the columns of Pierre Laval's newspaper, Le Moniteur. In the editorial pages those responsible for the defeat of France are sought out, and discovered: ''Let us be French; too many foreign influences have fed our misfortunes''—June 26th, 1940. Rene Mons, mason, is sentenced to three months in jail for defeatism. Editorial: ''Those responsible must be put on trial—the real reasons for our misfortunes must be analyzed.''

Pierre Laval.

26.

Pages from Le Moniteur. At top, the front page of July 11, 1940. At bottom, editorial: "Let us be French . . ."

Xenophobia, Anglophobia, anti-Semitism are found
throughout the editorials. The acquisition of French
nationality becomes more difficult. In Vichy, new decrees
are announced. ''The French elites must be restored.'' On
the same day, July 29th, 1940, Antoine Labonne, sausage-
maker in Clermont, is fined for having sold contaminated
ham.

**In those days did you ever discuss what the newspapers
were printing?**

MARCEL VERDIER, pharmacist in Clermont:
Never. We lived in closed circles—the one quality
we all shared was prudence. We had no idea what
the baker or the dairy man or the engineer or the
intellectual thought—we had no idea at all. So
everyone stood his guard.

**What was the main preoccupation of people at that time
according to you?**

MARCEL VERDIER:
Food. Food!

**Did it become the main preoccupation?**

MARCEL VERDIER:
Well, yes, it really did. There was secret slaughtering.
You had to have a bit of meat to survive, didn't you?
You know that the Frenchman is clever, that he loves
to scrounge a bit—so he had to try to get a little
more bread than his usual rationing; he had to get
a little more tobacco by smiling to his tobacconist;
he had to have a bit more of everything. Every
Saturday and Sunday a stream of bicycle riders
headed out to the country for provisions. There was
a system of coupons, of cards and restrictions. For
example, I was a smoker, and for me it was a terrible
thing not to have any cigarettes. It was awful, you
know—you were tempted to do anything: steal,
anything. When I had nothing else to smoke I even
plucked Jerusalem artichokes and rolled them. Since
it's my business I can say that, medically speaking,
kids born in that period between 1942 and 1944 ought
to have been undernourished and therefore
susceptible to rickets. But in fact it's quite the
opposite: These girls have a brother born in 1942,
and he is six feet three. For fear of giving him too

little, we fed him so much that he became a sort of giant. He is a great tennis player, and he studies architecture. . . but he is a giant.

Interminable lines are a sign of the food scarcity during the occupation. At top, lines in front of a dairy shop. At bottom, lining up in front of the butcher's.

To avoid lines at the butcher's, customers are asked to register for a number.

Do you think you fit the description of what is called a ''bourgeois'' in a large provincial town?

MARCEL VERDIER:
If being bourgeois consists of eating your fill, going hunting in the Sologne, owning a shooting place in Sanscoin and another in Serye, a pond in Sanscoin and having a son-in-law who owns a lake in Montcinère, then I am a bourgeois.

**When did you begin to feel the consequences of this period, that is, the persecutions? How could you feel something like that happening?**

MARCEL VERDIER :
In any case we felt nothing before '42. The only event I can remember was that, before the children arrived in September '42, the hunting season was opened again.

**Well, that's quite an event!**

MARCEL VERDIER :
It *was* an event, especially for the hunters. Game had accumulated for two years and there was plenty of it. It was very satisfying for those who had a gun.

FRENCH NEWSREEL, *film from government campaign to encourage raising of rabbits at home for food and clothing:*
*How sweet those little rabbits in their little nests! A few years ago I hated rabbit hutches and despised those darling little friends I have grown so fond of. Let's think about it—a rabbit! First of all it is the cook's joy, and while its skin hangs on the branches, the whole family rejoices.*

*Why not join me and raise rabbits? I love; you love; we love bunnies in all kinds of ways!*

GEORGES BIDAULT, former President of the National Resistance Council :
Usually the French are really not too concerned about politics. Suddenly they may take the bit in their teeth and. . . take the Bastille, or fight religious wars for fifty years, or make the French Revolution, or set off on the conquest of Europe. But generally, they are as peaceful a people as any other. What is certain is that the French in general like a peaceful regime, a strong regime, if possible a humane regime also. But at any rate they feel a certain need for protection. They are, in truth, paternalists.

**Is that how you would explain Petainism?**

GEORGES BIDAULT :
Of course. Let me add that I was in the French army,

with the noble rank of sergeant, and I know what it means to be routed. It is not a pretty sight.

JACQUES DUCLOS, Communist Party Chief during occupation:
Besides, one has to admit that Pétain was extraordinarily popular for a time. He was thought of as a good old man—you know, a little senile maybe, but after all, he had made France the gift of his person. It was quite a good formula, you know. I don't know if he thought it up himself, but it was quite good. The people could say: "He can't hurt anyone, that old man, he can only serve the cause of France. At his age, what can he hope for beyond that?" There were all sorts of arguments, all on that pretty low level, but they were still quite effective.

Marshal Pétain in Paris, 1944.

32.

FRENCH NEWSREEL :
*Marshal Pétain is fêted by French crowds.*
[Maurice Chevalier sang in 1942:]

*Quand on a roulé sur la
terre entière
On meurt d'envie du
retour dans le train
Le nez au carreau,
d'ouvrir la portière
Et d'embrasser tout
comme du bon pain,
Ce vieux clocher dans le
soleil couchant,
Ça sent si bon la France!
Ces grands blés mûrs
emplis de fleurs des
champs,
Ce jardinet où l'on voit
"chien méchant,"
Ça sent si bon la France!
A chaque gare un
murmure en
passant vous saisit
"Paris direct en
voiture,"
Oh! Ça sent bon le pays!
Et tout doucement, la vie
recommence
On s'était promis de tout
avaler,
Mais les rêves bleus, les
projets immenses,
Pour quelques jours on
les laisse filer . . .
Cette brunette aux yeux
de paradis,
Ça sent si bon la France!
Le PMU qui ferme avant
midi,
Le petit bar où l'on vous
fait crédit,
Ça sent si bon la France!
C'est samedi, faut plus
s'en faire,
Repos jusqu'à lundi
Belotte, r'b'lotte, dix deder,
Oh, ça sent bon le pays
Mais oui
Ça sent bon notre pays!*

*After a long trip all over
the world
In the train going back
home,
I feel like opening the
window
And hugging that old
steeple in the sunset.
It feels so good, it's
France!
This wheat field full of
wildflowers
This tiny garden with
its "Beware of dogs"
It feels so good, it's
France!
At every station you can
hear
"Paris Express, all
aboard"
Oh, it feels so good, it's
home!
And little by little life
comes back
We thought we were
going to win it all
But all our dreams, our
big projects,
We let them go for a
while.
This pretty brunette
with paradise eyes
It feels so good, it's
France!
The betting office which
closes at noon
The friendly little bar
still good for credit,
It feels so good, it's
France!
It's Saturday, throw
away your cares
Take a rest until Monday
Oh, it feels so good, it's
home!
Yes, our home!*

Gas masks become an everyday sight in Paris during '39-40.

34.

British bombardment of the Richelieu in Dakar, which followed their attack on Mers-el-Kébir. See Appendix B.

ROGER TOUNZE, newspaperman in Clermont:
Well truly, I was saddened by Mers-el-Kébir. At the time I was working in the Chantier de Jeunesse. I heard about it fifteen days after it happened and I didn't understand, I could not understand what had happened. Even now, after reading a lot of books on Mers-el-Kébir, I still don't understand it. It has always been a mystery.

CHARLES BRAUN, restaurant owner in Clermont:
Exactly, Mers-el-Kébir is a mystery.

**When you say mystery, do you mean the motives of the English are a mystery to you? You don't know why they did it?**

CHARLES BRAUN:
No, I never understood the English very well.

SIR EDWARD SPEARS, wartime liaison between
Churchill and de Gaulle:
On leaving Churchill—I was then a Member of
Parliament—I picked up my car from the House of
Commons and drove through Hyde Park and, there
in the middle of the park, I saw a group of French
sailors with those litle red pompoms on their caps
running about and playing with some English girls.
They ran, they played and shouted, and they
couldn't understand each other at all. I was
delighted. And then suddenly I felt horrible. I was
lucky not to crash my car, because suddenly I
remembered the ultimatum I had just read at
Churchill's office, and I thought of those French
ships at Mers-el-Kébir, where there were other
sailors, also with caps and little red pompoms—and
I wondered what would happen to them tomorrow.

FRENCH NEWSREELS, *Mers-el-Kébir—wounded sailors,
cannonfire, crying widows:*
*Here are the victims of the most repulsive and
outrageous aggression ever perpetrated. France's
former ally displays her strength only when she
believes she will find no resistance.*

36.

Page opposite: Admiral Darlan. Above: On the first anniversary of Mers-el Kébir, Marshal Pétain, Admiral Darlan, and General Huntziger leave ceremony in Vichy held to commemorate the French sailors killed in the attack.

In the morning, a few hours before the dramatic event, Admiral Gensoul had received the British ultimatum. Then, successively, several delegations from Admiral Somerville came to explain the various options envisioned by Winston Churchill the previous evening: 1) join the Free French; 2) permit disarmament; 3) go to a neutral port beyond the threat of the Germans.

Admiral Gensoul had refused these options, which he considered incompatible with his honor as a French sailor.

ANTHONY EDEN, former Prime Minister of Great Britain:
What we didn't dare to risk happening was that those ships should pass at any foreseeable stage under

German control . . . that would have had the most
deplorable consequences for the whole of our chance
of winning the war. That was at stake. And so we
just simply couldn't take the risk.

**But the risk on the other hand was very heavy
psychologically speaking wasn't it, I mean, it gave the
Germans a propaganda weapon of some size?**

ANTHONY EDEN:
And Vichy too. And they used it. I think we knew
that. I mean I think we understood that. But in this
choice of difficulties we thought, there was no doubt
to our minds, where the balance lay.

CHRISTIAN DE LA MAZIERE:
Sixteen hundred sailors were killed by the British
navy, you cannot get around that. The British navy
had tried to seize the French navy : it was quite
obvious for us at the time. We thought, we supposed,
that the armistice would be respected by the
Germans. France thought, because the Vichy
government had said so, that the French navy
would never be handed over to the Germans. Vichy
had given its word of honor that it would be so. For
us it was a fact. I was brought up to respect the
word of honor; I never imagined for a moment that
there might be political bargaining which would
bring French ships into action. It was unthinkable.
So for us the British attack was a brutal aggression.

**There was also a moral problem. It has been said in various
accounts that the sailors who received the British shells on
their ships thought they were preparing to join the British
fleet.**

ANTHONY EDEN:
It is a terrible thing. If there had been any hope at
all of that, obviously we would not have done it, but
in our opinion there was no hope.

SIR EDWARD SPEARS, wartime liaison between
Churchill and de Gaulle:
The proof of what we said about the Germans was
proved at Bizerta. The Germans gave the French
admiral twenty minutes to surrender, ships and all,
under the threat of being attacked and taken

prisoner. We were right in our predictions. We knew who we were dealing with.

GENERAL WALTER WARLIMONT, former aide to Supreme Command of the Wehrmacht:
It was at that time and as a result of these events that the French, who felt quite shaken in their loyalty towards England, developed their first contacts with us through General Huntziger, at the Armistice Commission in Wiesbaden. They wondered if there could not be some new clauses added to the armistice to deal with questions of common military collaboration. And the negotiations which led to what is now referred to as "collaboration" started with those possibilities, which each side probably proposed for quite different reasons. At the beginning of this new turn of events there took place the meeting of Hitler and Pétain at Montoire.

October 24, 1940: Pétain and Hitler meet at Montoire. Standing between them is Paul Schmidt.

PAUL SCHMIDT, Hitler's chief interpreter:
Laval stated at once, on the very first meeting, that
he was pro-German. And since he had known me for
a while he asked me to speak on his behalf to Hitler,
which I did. I believe Hitler felt that Laval was at
least partly sincere when he spoke of collaboration—
which was the main item on the agenda at the second
meeting. Usually, in such a situation, those defeated
want to know what will happen to them. Pétain
asked, for example, in which language the peace
treaty would be written. As for the victors—I've
often observed them—they usually don't have any
idea what to do next, and are not yet ready to
respond to this sort of question. And this is precisely
what happened at Montoire. Hitler did not know
how to answer Pétain's questions about the dividing
line or about the future of French prisoners. So all
in all the meeting ended with everything still up in
the air.

ROGER TOUNZE, newspaperman in Clermont:
The Montoire meeting! That was something! First of
all no one knew where Montoire was. We all had to
look it up in the dictionary to find out; then later
when we heard the outcome of the meeting, we didn't
exactly feel overjoyed. The next day people were
crying over it.

**Some people were crying?**

ROGER TOUNZE:
Yes they were. And then all at once someone came
up with this slogan, I don't know who:
"Collaboration, it's..."

CHARLES BRAUN, restaurant owner in Clermont:
"... give me your watch and I'll tell you the time."

ROGER TOUNZE:
That's right, that's how it went.

GENERAL WALTER WARLIMONT, former aide to
Supreme Command of the Wehrmacht:
According to Hitler's plans, France was to have a
minor role in the New Europe, led by Germany. He
told me as much several times. Besides, because of
the race ideology, he preferred the British to the

French. He was not a well-travelled man. He picked up his ideas on France from books that were probably biased and which he never bothered to question. Thus he pictured a decadent France that would go on declining forever.

July 1, 1940: German poster pasted up over French poster in an appeal to refugees: ''Trust in the German soldier!''

GERMAN NEWSREEL, *Hitler's train on its way through southwestern France:*

During his trips, Chancellor Adolf Hitler sometimes shares his most intimate thoughts with close friends.

April 5th, 1942. Dinner.

The Führer explains that, in politics, if one has decided to violate a written agreement, there is no point in

quibbling over details. That is why the French must be
watched at all times to prevent them from acting in bad
faith. It would be silly for them to try to pick the pockets
of an old professional like the Fuhrer himself. In any case,
the task which now faces France for the next fifty years
is to work hard at making good the injustice done at
Versailles.

April 24th, 1942. Evening meal.

The Fuhrer declares that he is not inclined to grant
requests from members of the Wehrmacht to marry foreign
girls in the occupied territories. Generally such requests
are generated by the scarcity of sexual opportunity
suffered by our occupying troops. In viewing the
photographs included with the requests, he is struck by the
contrast between the German soldiers and the women, who
are generally misshapen, misbegotten, and rather pitiful
looking. The Fuhrer feels that such marriages are condemned
in advance, not only for reasons of personal happiness,
but for reasons of racial purity as well. He would be more
inclined to favor harmless, brief affairs, which are probably
inevitable in such a situation.

GENERAL WALTER WARLIMONT :
Conditions created by the pressure of the National-
Socialist machine within the structure of German
society of the time meant that the armistice
conditions could not be respected by our side. We
were not able to prevent this disintegration of the
armistice agreements, nor to prevent the many things
which still disturb anyone with any feeling or
thought. We were unable to prevent Hitler and the
party apparatus from incorporating Alsace-Lorraine
into the Third Reich, installing *Gauleiters,* and
finally drafting the young men of Alsace-Lorraine
into the Wehrmacht. All this was beyond our power,
and you can blame us as much as you like, until
doomsday if you wish—we could not prevent any of
it.

AT A WEDDING IN GERMANY, 1969:

You mentioned that after you were wounded in Russia,
you were sent to Alsace, and then to France. Why do you
mention Alsace first. Wasn't that part of France?

HELMUT TAUSEND, Captain of the Wehrmacht in
Clermont :
No. We did not regard it as French territory. The

people were pro-German. I asked all my family to
join me there. Of course there were some ill-disposed
people there, some patriot types capable of anything,
but there weren't many of them. I felt I was in an
old German country.

**And today?**

HELMUT TAUSEND:
Well, I haven't been back there.

**But what is your opinion of Alsace today?**

HELMUT TAUSEND:
My opinion? Well, I think it's still true: Alsace is
part of Germany.

GERMAN NEWSREEL:
*And here, a comradely stage show in the rest quarters
of the Waffen S.S. Bruno Fritz performs his
hilarious Ice Hockey Routine.*

FRENCH NEWSREEL:
*One hundred thousand French workers are now
working in Germany, contributing to the economic
collaboration between France and Germany. Every
week four trains leave Paris for the big industrial
centers of Germany. Today at the Gare du Nord,
Doctor Elmar Michel, German Economic Adviser,
has come in person to shake hands with the 100,000th
French worker: Monsieur Edouard Lefebvre.*

*"Well, Monsieur Lefebvre, so you are the man of the
day. Were you unemployed?"*

*"Yes. I had been for quite a while."*

*"For how long?"*

*"Well, about two years."*

*"Are you a married man? Do you have many
children?"*

*"Yes, I am married. I have small children."*

*"Take your seats, the train is leaving!"*

*This giant organization has already brought many
happy results: the fight against unemployment,
and mutual understanding between workers of both
countries.*

Monsieur Lefebvre, 100,000th French worker to leave for Germany, shakes hands with Dr. Elmar Michel.

ELMAR MICHEL, head of Economic Division, German
Occupation Forces:
Since 1923 I had been on the staff of the German
Ministry of Economics. The Secretary of State, Herr
Lansfried, notified me in June 1940, to go to Paris
and become the head of the Economic Department
in the military headquarters of occupied France.
He was anxious to forestall some bureaucrat within
the National-Socialist Party from taking that post.

**Were you not yourself a member of the Party?**

ELMAR MICHEL:
Yes, I was. I had joined the Party a short while
earlier, also at Herr Lansfried's request. We tried
to reconcile the sensible with the possible. We
wanted to act as fairly as possible, in order to serve
French interests as well as German interests.

44.

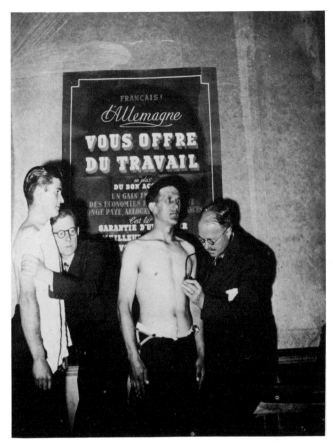

Medical examinations are given volunteer workers leaving for Germany.

GERMAN NEWSREEL:

*This much-praised democracy, in its twenty years of blind victory frenzy, was never in condition to eliminate this type of miserable slum housing. The National-Socialist nation endeavors to provide clean and attractive homes for workers of both mind and of body throughout its Empire.*

*Here is a new settlement in the small industrial site of Lauta. Of course within the settlement can be found a kindergarten and nurses' station, a day care center for mother and child, and an X-ray laboratory. . . .*

German poster in Paris advertising victory over the Bolsheviks: ''The triumph of Germany who is fighting for a New Europe.''

Somehow one gets the feeling, when looking at German newsreels, that there was a certain kind of rather openly racial propaganda which implied that the German talent for organization and discipline was required in order to bring about cleanliness and tidiness within this French confusion.

ELMAR MICHEL:
Yes, you are quite right. There was a propaganda department in Paris, but it was controlled from Berlin. May I point out that one of the first visits paid to me by the French government, at least on the ministerial level, was from the Minister of Communications in September of 1940. He came accompanied by the owner of a large racing stables, to ask me for authorization for the reopening of horse racing at Longchamps and Auteuil—since it served a real need of the people.

46.

July 1941: Fashionable ladies at the race track for the ''Journée des drags.''

GERMAN NEWSREEL, *at the race track:*
*Attendance at the races is better than ever before.*
*No more doubt about it—Paris has found herself*
*again!*

ELMAR MICHEL:
I discussed the matter with my associates and we
said: Why not? Horse racing started again, and there
were races in Paris regularly until 1944.

NEWSREEL, *The Opéra in Paris—finale of an*
*operetta, curtain, audience applauding.*

ELMAR MICHEL:
Thanks to us the theaters were also opened. They
were very busy. You either went alone or with
friends. Of course the Germans went to the races.
And this is how the French and the Germans were

June 1943, fashion at the races: the Grand Prix de Paris held at Trembley.

able to meet; in fact, personal relations between different people on all sides could take place there, no doubt with differing motives.

You know of course that in France, post-war myths have led people to deny that any such personal contact ever took place.

ELMAR MICHEL:
Yes but they did.

CHRISTIAN DE LA MAZIERE, former volunteer in French Waffen S.S.:

Engagez-vous...

...à la Waffen-SS

Werbestelle (Bureau de recrutement): LILLE, rue Faidherbes, 14.

Recruitment poster for the French Waffen SS.

And Germany was triumphant. Wherever her armies went they were victorious. I must say that the German army at that time made a great impression on young people. The sight of those German soldiers, stripped to the waist.... Let me remind you, if I may, that I am the son of a soldier, I am a soldier myself, and I had in me a great sense of responsibility, of hierarchy, discipline. A disciplined army is very important for people like us.

For the first time we saw an army which was all we had dreamed ours might be. The French army was made up of rather sloppy recruits—not exactly the kind of soldier that puts fear into the heart of the mob. It is a terrible thing to say, but it must be said. It is the truth.

FRENCH NEWSREEL, *teenagers in uniform outside at youth camp assembly:*

*The oath of the Vichy army:*
           *We swear to unite,*
           *and to gather all our forces,*
           *our faith, our ardor,*
           *at the service of the Marshal,*
           *at the service of France.*

*During three days spent together, these young people have showed their desire for discipline and unity*

August 1941 in Marcherois: exercises with shovel being performed in the irrigation yard of a rural center.

*towards their leader. They now spend the evening*
*around the campfire singing: "Up there on the*
*mountain. . . ."*

SIR EDWARD SPEARS, wartime liaison between
Churchill and de Gaulle:
The French strongly believe in the military, and in
the end they always turn to the military, whether it
be to restore order, or for fear of a coup d'état, or to
*carry out* a coup d'état—but they always end up with
their soldier, with his cap, his pompom, his sword,
whether he be the supply captain or anyone else.
They have a taste for rank in France.

FRENCH NEWSREEL, *poem by Gendarme C. Languillon,*
*published in* Le Moniteur, *page one, on November*
*24th 1940:*

His name rings out like a shot
Pétain! He is full of energy and good will, his soul is ready,

August 1941 at La Chapelle-en-Serval: young people at a
Camp de Jeunesse take the oath to support Marshal Pétain.

but kindness has always preserved him from being haughty.
This great victor who is even greater in defeat.

Schemers, foreigners, jugglers and cretins
have brought you close to death, O France!
The victor of Verdun, brushing aside these puppets,
cleans up our house from top to bottom.
Herculean labor, bitter recovery.
And from the ruins can be heard the muffled gruntings
of former profiteers, buried in the rubble.

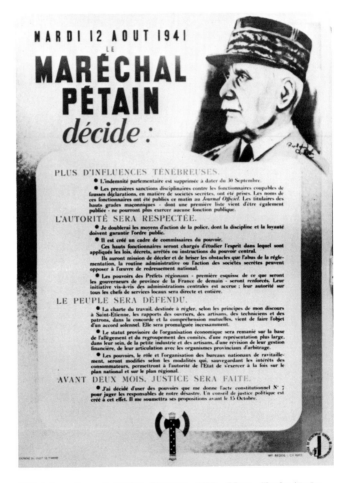

Official poster of Vichy France: ''No More Shady Influences,'' ''Authority Shall be Respected,'' ''The People shall be Defended,'' ''Within Two Months Justice Shall Be Done.''

CHRISTIAN DE LA MAZIERE, former volunteer in
French Waffen S.S.:
In a series of speeches, Pétain analyzed the reasons
for our defeat. He described them very cleverly; it
was very appealing. If you were to re-read those
texts now—I myself haven't re-read them, it no longer
interests me—but I think that if you took the trouble
to re-read them, you would be amazed.

**Yes, they certainly played upon the collective subconscious of the time.**

**Vichy poster: ''Buy Treasury Bonds.''**

Vichy poster    "1941: the Year of the Clean-up!"

CHRISTIAN DE LA MAZIERE:
That's it. Absolutely. The scapegoats were politicians,
democratic politicians; a certain kind of alien shop
owner—shady, foreign, cosmopolitan; and of course
the Communist Party, which was the cause of all
misfortunes.

COLONEL R. DU JONCHAY, former resister, of
monarchist leanings:
All the hotels were requisitioned, and the Hotel du
Parc was occupied by Marshal Pétain. There I met

54.

my good friend, Colonel de Goroztardu, who lived with the Marshal. He was head of aviation in the Vichy government.

**Yes.**

COLONEL R. DU JONCHAY:
So I often came to the Hotel du Parc. It was swarming with people. But everyone spoke in a hushed voice, watching each other. Since I was not used to this, I spoke normally: "What?"... "Shush, lower your voice, be quiet!" They were all on their guard.

**On guard against the enemy or against each other?**

COLONEL R. DU JONCHAY:
A bit of both.

**Are you a republican?**

COLONEL R. DU JONCHAY:
Not very.

Bastille Day 1941 in Vichy: Marshal Pétain, Admiral Darlan, and General Dentz.

**Not very?**

COLONEL R. DU JONCHAY:
No.

**More of a monarchist?**

COLONEL R. DU JONCHAY:
Yes, more of a monarchist.

FRENCH NEWSREEL, *end of 1940:*
*Monsieur Gonthier de Basse, sergeant-*
*pilot, veteran of the First World War, volunteer in*
*'39, wounded at Dunkirk, has decided to make the*
*following statement, of his own free will:*

*"Since I returned from England on*
*the hospital ship* Sphinx *on the 5th of October,*
*I have been amazed by the number of my fellow*
*Frenchmen who still believe that soldiers wounded*
*at Warwick and Dunkirk have all been well treated*
*by our former ally. I have decided to publish my*
*unhappy experience. When we arrived in England,*
*we bore no prejudice towards our English comrades.*
*But after the tragic events of June, when we were*
*asked to serve under another flag, when we were*
*given bonus payments and paid in pounds Sterling,*
*we could do no less than express our contempt and*
*our indignation. For we French soldiers could*
*serve only under our own colors, and it would have*
*been treason to act otherwise.*

*"Frenchmen, comrades, it is our duty to follow our*
*leader, Marshal Pétain, to restore our defeated*
*France to her place in a New Europe, so that our*
*French prisoners may return home soon. The task*
*ahead of us is a hard one. Those who divide us are*
*our enemies. Let us unite. Let us be disciplined."*

SIR EDWARD SPEARS, wartime liaison between
Churchill and de Gaulle:
Their idea was to get out of the war no matter what,
as quickly as possible. We had 15,000 French sailors
at Liverpool. I went to speak to them. I tried to
persuade them to continue the fighting. Impossible.
We were so short of men that we asked them to dig
trenches. We even offered them wages. They refused.
They said: "France is out of the war, we don't even
have the right to dig trenches." You see the sort of
attitude. . . .

At top, August 17, 1940 at Dormans (Marne): German soldiers glue up anti-British poster. At bottom: Anti-British poster: ''The New Europe will arise from which England and Russia will be excluded. England will be chased into the seas and Tartar Russia into the Steppes.'' —Victor Hugo.

Anti-British poster: ''The assassins always return to the sites of their crimes.''

**Yes.**

SIR EDWARD SPEARS:
This blind stubbornness to get out at all costs. . .

**Yes.**

SIR EDWARD SPEARS:
As for what might happen to England, they couldn't have cared less. That was the way it was—we were defeated, and if the French army was defeated, it was impossible to imagine that the English would survive.

58.

Announcement of the trial of Mendès-France, Zay, Viénot, and Wiltzer on charges of desertion stemming out of the Massilia incident. From Le Moniteur.

On June 17th, 1940, an ocean liner, the Massilia, leaves Bordeaux for Morocco. On board are many members of Parliament. The departure will cause a great deal of ink to flow.

PIERRE MENDES-FRANCE, former Prime Minister of France:
I embarked on the *Massilia* never dreaming the *Massilia* would become a trap. But quite soon the politicians who had remained in Bordeaux realized that they could exploit this and present the departure of the *Massilia*, with a number of politicians on board, as a sign of panic—an escape, a surrender. . .

Runaways. . .

PIERRE MENDES-FRANCE:
Yes, finally. Runaways—in the final analysis, deserters. The people on the *Massilia*, who were really the people who wanted to fight, were quickly judged as cowards and runaways. And paradoxically a certain number of them—Vienot, Jean Zay, and myself—were charged with desertion, when their idea

had been to go on fighting. And as far as I was
concerned, it was my duty to go, since my unit was
headed there and I had to follow and rejoin it.


COLONEL R. DU JONCHAY, former resister, of
monarchist leanings:
So everyone met in Rabat. It was awfully crowded.
I went to lunch at the "Balima" which was the big
restaurant in Rabat where everybody met. One of
my cousins was there. He is a flyer and we were
discussing the latest events. He pointed out
Mendès-France, who was having lunch with a
charming woman, who was his wife, and my cousin
said: "There is one of the men responsible for our
defeat; he was the Secretary of State for Aviation."
And this little secretary, this little lieutenant, was
drinking champagne! Well, really, the champagne
threw me into a rage. So I went over and told him
that this was not the right attitude after the defeat,
to drink champagne in public as though he were
delighted by what had happened.

**And then?**

COLONEL R. DU JONCHAY:
I told him that if I saw him again I would throw him
out, and I gave him my card. There was quite a fuss
about it.

**It was almost a way of provoking a duel?**

COLONEL R. DU JONCHAY:
Oh no. I gave him my card simply to show him who I
was, so as not to conceal my identity.

**And what was his reaction?**

COLONEL R. DU JONCHAY:
He stood at attention and said nothing. I was a
captain, he was a lieutenant.


PIERRE MENDES-FRANCE:
I have mentioned capitulation. I have mentioned
treason. It was clear that something else was
beginning to appear: anti-Semitism. People who
would not have dared admit their anti-Semitism
before were suddenly beginning to proclaim it. Since

they were beginning to absorb German principles and to seek a closer understanding with Hitler—a conception of a future Europe in which France and Germany would collaborate—it was obvious that anti-Semitism provided a bond between certain German elements and certain French elements. Well, of course, Jean Zay and I had the misfortune to be Jews. Well actually, I was—Jean Zay was only part Jewish, in fact his father had been a convert, but at any rate he was of Jewish origin. That didn't prevent them from starting a campaign against him, a horrible campaign of hate, which ended only once he had been murdered.

Jean Zay was arrested. His wife was in Casablanca, and she was pregnant. She had terrible difficulties, it should be mentioned, in finding a hospital bed or an obstetrician. There was so much hatred that when they found out it was Madame Zay, no one had the courage to admit her to a maternity ward or a clinic. You cannot imagine the prejudice at that time. The pregnancy of Madame Zay was very difficult. She was living with my wife at the time, and they both suffered some very cruel moments where both of them were treated very badly. My wife alone also had some very hard, very painful moments. Finally Madeleine Zay had a baby, and I saw it, because I was arrested after the baby was born. So when I was transferred to the prison at Clermont-Ferrand, where I found Jean Zay, I had seen his daughter, and he had not as yet.


MAITRE HENRI ROCHAT, lawyer in Clermont:
We were forced to deal with a magistrate named Colonel Leprêtre. I don't usually mention names but that one I will mention because he has remained famous in the military court of Clermont-Ferrand.

PIERRE MENDES-FRANCE:
He was very intelligent, very cunning and subtle, clever, with an element of repressing perversity—of hatred for any prisoner. Even more so if the prisoner was a left-winger or an important man. He found a sort of morbid pleasure in it. Apart from interrogations, he would come to the prison occasionally and chat with prisoners. He would enter the cell, sit down on the bed, and pretend to speak in a straightforward manner. He clearly enjoyed

holding men in his power, especially men who had once been important. It was really something very unhealthy, very peculiar. A strange character.

Pierre Mendès-France.

**And did he grow confidential when he was relaxed?**

PIERRE MENDES-FRANCE:
He told me one day: "Oh I know what you think of me." He was intelligent enough to understand perfectly, he was really very intelligent. One day he told me: "I know very well what you think of me. In an organized society there are a certain number of tasks which must be carried out, and there must be men to assume them. There must be garbage collectors in every society." He used the term himself.

**Were you able to bring out any of the political or racial undertones during the trial?**

MAITRE HENRI ROCHAT:
No. We wanted to get our client acquitted, and we were not dealing with judges who would have been sensitive to that kind of argument. And although we did say that our client's being Jewish should have no relevance to the case, we still had no illusions. We knew very well that it would have relevance.

And the session was a stormy one. It began at nine in the morning with a declaration by Mendès-France, whom the presiding colonel treated with blatant contempt. He had been given a little table and a carafe of water. He began with this statement: "My colonel, gentlemen: I am a Jew, I am a Freemason, but I am not a deserter. Now let the trial begin."

PIERRE MENDES-FRANCE:
The tribunal was presided over by a rather frenetic character called Colonel Perret, who was in the tank corps and held a particular hatred for General de Gaulle, because they had been... I think they were in Saint-Cyr together, and they had been in competition with each other. Everything to do with de Gaulle, or Gaullism, or that was Gaullist, was fuel for his hatred. Furthermore he was uncontrolled, a frantic character who held his hearings in an abominable manner. The fact that he convicted me is not the worst that can be said of him. In other cases he condemned men to death; he was responsible for executions—and that is infinitely worse than what happened to me.

MAITRE HENRI ROCHAT:
I must say that from the very beginning the spectators in the court were extremely hostile. Let's call things by their name: the audience had been packed...

PIERRE MENDES-FRANCE:
... women with hate on their faces. Now I won't mention names, but really awful people, people who were hoping for a vicious condemnation, who were sorry that I was not shot at once, who regretted even that I was allowed to speak in my own defense....

MAITRE HENRI ROCHAT:
I think about three or four hundred admission cards

had been sent out; there were six for the defense.

PIERRE MENDES-FRANCE:
An amusing detail: since only a certain number of
admission cards had been distributed and they were
very much in demand, a kind of strange black market
developed. There were bars in Clermont where tickets
could be bought. It was quite flattering actually,
because the price was relatively high—twenty francs
for a show was at that time more expensive than
the movies!

MAITRE HENRI ROCHAT:
Public opinion was obviously manipulated by the
Vichy press—those newspapers which used to
proclaim the guilt of political prisoners before their
trials had even begun.

PIERRE MENDES-FRANCE:
Well my colonel came as witness, and then my
lieutenant colonel, then my general—all the people to
whom I was subordinate. And all of them testified
that I had not deserted.

MAITRE HENRI ROCHAT:
When the prosecutor—whose name I won't mention
either—told him in a rather shaky voice that he was
sentenced to six years in prison for desertion, Mendès
replied: "Well sir, I suppose you will get your Iron
Cross, you have worked very well for your master!"

PIERRE MENDES-FRANCE:
A man came the next day to see Rochat—I don't
know if Rochat has told you this—and he told him:
"I am a Pétainist, and I am insulted by what I have
seen here today. It is awful, a scandal. The Marshal
cannot know that such things are happening; he is
being deceived; he must be informed at once! I
saw that you were having a shorthand transcript
made"—which was correct—"could you give me a
copy to bring to the Marshal myself?" Rochat of
course provided the man with a copy which was sent to
the Marshal; and of course nothing came of it. And
the man who took this step was a minister of state
called Giscard d'Estaing—father of our present
Minister of Finance.

FRENCH NEWSREEL, *inside elementary schoolroom:*
*The Marshal has come to speak to these children and*
*to their brothers, to all the little children of the*
*schools of France, in whom he sees the country's*
*hope. He speaks simply to them as he knows how, in*
*the humble school of the village of Périgny.*

*"Well, now you are going to sit down, since*
*you mustn't have to listen to me standing up.*
*Young schoolchildren of France! The reason I*
*wanted to speak to you today as you are beginning*
*a new school year, is that I wanted you to know*
*that I am counting on you to help me in rebuilding*
*France. To work! Be strong and get good marks!"*

[The children sing "La Marseillaise."]

Mother's Day in Vichy: Marshal Pétain is welcomed by children.

GEORGES LAMIRAND, Secretary of Youth, under Pétain:

As I told you, when I passed through Vichy on my way to Billancourt at the beginning of August '40, people told me: "You know the Marshal is very tired out, he is lucid only two hours a day." So I was amazed to meet this old man, still straight as an arrow, with the marmoreal gaze people have often noticed, who put me at ease with extraordinary grace. He had me sit down; he welcomed me with a great courtesy and said: "But Monsieur Lamirand, many people have been talking about you lately in our little capital. . . ."

Georges Lamirand in 1969.

FRENCH NEWSREEL:
*Secretary of Youth Lamirand visited during a tour today Lavalette Camp, the training camp of leaders*

*of the future Chantiers de Jeunesse, where tomor-
row's young people will be shaped. He witnessed
groups of young men, leading a simple life in
constant contact with nature, work, and simplicity—
those foundations upon which the country must be
rebuilt.*

GEORGES LAMIRAND:
We chatted for a while, and I thought to myself:
I've got all the luck! I am told he is lucid only two
hours a day and I happen to come during those two
hours! I am very interested in the problems of youth,
but I did not realize that a job like the one Marshal
Pétain wanted to offer me could have so many
exciting aspects, and so many serious problems to
solve.

FRENCH NEWSREEL; *Lamirand addressing rally:*
*"Young people! all after me: Long live France!"*
*"Long live France!"*
*"And long live the Marshal!"*
*"Long live the Marshal!"*

The young Georges Lamirand, Secretary of Youth for Vichy,
addressing a rally.

GEORGES LAMIRAND:
Louis Renault who was my employer in Billancourt,
finally approved of my commission and told the

67.

Marshal: "Listen, I'll lend him to you for a month."
And the Marshal added with great wit and subtlety:
"Yes a month, if you will, Monsieur Renault—
renewable." And he renewed my appointment thirty
times.

Poster from the Office of the Secretary of Youth: "The New
France—For Us Youth." Notice the francisque, a hatchet
used by the ancient Gauls, appropriated by Vichy as a symbol of traditional values.

FRENCH NEWSREEL:
*At the Musée Galliera, Monsieur Lamirand opens an
exhibit of drawings sent to Marshal Pétain by the
schoolchildren of France. Little children from all
over wanted to respond to the challenge. They
wanted to show the Marshal the drawings of their
city, their village, their house—to tell him through
pictures of their everyday life. A schoolgirl, perhaps
the youngest of all, is allowed to present in person
to the Marshal her own letter, which she wrote with
so much care and affection.*

GEORGES LAMIRAND:
The idea was to do something new, to do something
new along the lines of the famous three-headed
motto: "Work, Family, and Fatherland." To honor
work, and to honor the family, as well as the
Fatherland.

**And what about the national revolution?**

GEORGES LAMIRAND:
Nothing but a slogan!

FRENCH NEWSREEL, *Lamirand addressing rally:*
*"The Marshal has often explained what he
means by his social revolution. He holds the deep
conviction that we have lived in an unfair social
regime with too much misery and too many injustices.
Well, the Marshal wants to change this world! He
has the will and the determination to bring greater
happiness to France, and he asks everyone to share
in this common effort. That is, above all, the social
revolution of the Marshal!"*

MAITRE HENRI ROCHAT, lawyer in Clermont:
So then he began to prepare carefully for his escape.
He let his beard grow, then he shaved it off, then he
let it grow again, and then one day he just decided
to leave.

PIERRE MENDES-FRANCE, former Prime Minister of
France:
I must say that I am not very much of a sportsman,
but I prepared myself for this test by doing a lot of
exercise in the months preceding. So there I was, on
top of the wall; I had to jump, it was quite high and

it was risky, but at least then I would be free. Just
as I was about to jump—it was a tree-lined avenue
—I heard an unexpected noise, voices, and I tried
to distinguish shapes in the semi-darkness. There
was a couple under the tree. You can imagine what
they were talking about: he had a very definite
goal in mind; she couldn't decide one way or the
other. It took a very long time. She finally did say
yes—it seemed as if her resistance had been nearly
interminable. Then they left, and I jumped. And I
swear that at that moment I was happier than he
was. I would like to meet those two sometime. I'd
like to tell them how much I went through with
them that night.

**How his boldness pleased you. . .**

PIERRE MENDES-FRANCE:
And how untimely her lack of boldness seemed to me.
Well, finally love, luck and escape won out!

**Were you disguised?**

PIERRE MENDES-FRANCE:
I was disguised, not very heavily though. So many
people tried to disguise themselves by growing a
beard in that period that after a while beards
themselves became suspicious. I grew a moustache;
I parted my hair in the middle, I wore glasses, and I
dressed differently.

MAITRE HENRI ROCHAT:
The next day, making my daily visit, I wondered
whether or not he'd made it out. I arrived and saw
people with measuring sticks taking all kind of
measurements—very nervous people; they asked me,
"What do you want?" "I've come to see my client,"
I replied. "What client?" "Mendès-France" "You
want to see Mendès-France?" "Yes." "Don't you
know he has escaped?" "No kidding! he escaped?"
And so I started laughing, which they didn't like
at all. And then they started checking everything.
There were roadblocks, they alerted the trains. . . .

PIERRE MENDES-FRANCE:
My rule was never to speak to anyone, never to rely
on anyone, to remain cut off from everything. I must
say that it's difficult to imagine what life in France
was like at the time and very difficult to describe it.

September 1941: ''le taxi hippomobile'' in use in Paris during gasoline scarcity.

If an old pair of shoes needed a new sole, you
couldn't do anything about it because there was no
leather. There were no plates, there were no matches,
there wasn't anything, nothing. . . . It's really very
difficult to describe what life was like in a country
where everyone spent all their time looking for
things.

FRENCH NEWSREEL, *product demonstration inside
beauty shop:*
*The latest "find" in Paris is the silkless silk
stocking. The trick, ladies, is simply to paint your
legs. Just think about it—it's both easy and
practical. Already the most elegant ladies have
replaced the garter with the brush. But perhaps you,
sir, sit there smiling, thinking the paint will wash
off after the first bath? You are wrong, because
the painted stocking is waterproof, it does not fade,
and Elizabeth Arden guarantees that it will not run.*

FRENCH NEWSREEL:
*Where goes France? Where goes Europe? At the
Palais de Chaillot, Monsieur Alphonse de
Chateaubriand speaks to 3,000 people about the
French drama.*

*"At this very moment one can see the*
*outlines of a vast continental unit, a gigantic*
*demographic whole, forming one political and*
*economical entity which stretches as far as the*
*extreme point of Europe—represented by France.*
*From there the importance of France becomes*
*obvious, since France becomes in this way the*
*spearhead, the last bastion of this immense continent*
*on the Atlantic, facing across to the great American*
*continent which is getting ready to absorb the old*
*order, the old wealth and its capitalist credos, the*
*old gold and the old man, in order to become their*
*last fortress and their last army. I hope that all of*
*what I've said will open your eyes to the deep*
*meaning of the word 'collaboration'. . . ."*

PIERRE MENDES-FRANCE:
There is no doubt that at first these poisonous
arguments did some damage. However, people pulled
themselves together gradually. The very excess of
propaganda, and the fact that the government's
policy led blatantly to collaboration with the enemy,
gradually opened people's eyes. But that propaganda
still did some damage, since you know as well as I
do that anti-semitism and Anglophobia are two
things that can always be easily revived in France.
Even if such impulses are momentarily dim or
dormant, it only takes an event, an incident, an
international circumstance, a Dreyfus affair or
whatever, to bring them to life again, to suddenly
bring springing back things you thought were dead
but which were in fact merely inactive.

FRENCH NEWSREEL:
*This is the home of Edouard Drumont, the first man*
*in France to pose the Jewish problem with all of its*
*implications. The Institute for Jewish Affairs, in the*
*presence of his widow, celebrates the memory of this*
*courageous precursor. Monsieur Laville has been*
*kind enough to offer us a few words on this occasion.*

*"Ninety percent of those Frenchmen of old*
*French stock are true white men, free of any racial*
*mixture. This is not true of Jews. The Jew is the*
*product of the cross-breeding between Aryans,*
*Mongols, and Negroes which took place milleniums*
*ago. The Jew has therefore a face, a body, attitudes*
*and gestures which are peculiar to him. It is*
*encouraging to see that the public is keenly*

*interested in the study of their characteristics which*
*are presented in the morphological section of the*
*exhibition, 'The Jew and France.' ''*

Publicity outside hall announces the anti-semitic exhibition,
''The Jew and France,'' sponsored by the Institute for the
Study of Jewish Questions.

ROGER TOUNZE, newspaperman in Clermont:
In October, 1940, when I came home on leave from
the army—or maybe it was in November—I found
that a good friend of mine, a school teacher in the
lycée, had been prevented from returning to his

73.

teaching post on the first of October on the pretext that he was a Jew on his mother's side, and so half Jewish. I had known many Jews before him, but I never distinguished between them and Catholics or Protestants or people who had no religion. So then I began to get angry, to rebel; I started asking myself some questions. . . .

C'EST UNE NÉCESSITÉ POUR TOUT FRANÇAIS DÉCIDÉ A SE DÉFENDRE CONTRE L'EMPRISE HÉBRAÏQUE QUE D'APPRENDRE À RECONNAITRE LE JUIF

FAITES RAPIDEMENT VOTRE INSTRUCTION EN CONSULTANT CES DOCUMENTS.

From the exhibit "The Jew and France": "It is necessary that each Frenchman determined to defend himself against the Hebraic takeover learn to recognize the Jew. Instruct yourselves by consulting these documents."

**IN COURTYARD OF THE LYCEE PASCAL IN CLERMONT**

**Were there any Jewish teachers at your school?**

MONSIEUR DIONNET, librarian at Lycée Pascal in Clermont:
Yes, one. He was dismissed.

74.

MONSIEUR DANTON, teacher at Lycée Pascal in
Clermont:
He came...

MONSIEUR DIONNET:
Always the same—no one said a word.

MONSIEUR DANTON:
Well, if I may add a word, take the case of Never.
I think that we tried to find him some private
tutoring. The same went for another colleague who
had been dismissed. But as you say, it wasn't much;
but still I think there was some sympathy. Yes, there
was.

**When you say: "What could we do?" what do you mean?
Ultimately you could have offered a collective resignation
from the lycée couldn't you?**

MONSIEUR DIONNET:
Well, that was out of the question. You don't have
any understanding of teachers... collective
resignation, come on!

**In the fall of 1940, Vichy announced its Jewish laws. In
the classified section of Le Moniteur, a Clermont
shopkeeper notified his worthy customers that he was a
Frenchman, as were his ancestors before him.**

**Sir, are you Marius?**

MARIUS KLEIN, shopkeeper in Clermont:
Yes, I am Marius.

**I see you are wearing many decorations.**

MARIUS KLEIN:
Well, I am a veteran of the First World War.

**All those decorations stem from that time?**

MARIUS KLEIN:
Yes, they do.

**You must have been a very courageous man.**

MARIUS KLEIN:
Well, just like the others...

Yes.

MARIUS KLEIN:
I did my duty, that's all.

In 1940, after the defeat, how did you react?

MARIUS KLEIN:
Well, listen, we did not like it. We, as veterans of the First World War, we were deeply hurt by the defeat.

Yes. Were there many Jewish shops in this city?

MARIUS KLEIN:
Yes.

Then you must have seen many unpleasant things?

Outside the auction hall: "By order of the General Commission on Jewish Questions: the entrance of Jews into the auctions halls is strictly forbidden."

MARIUS KLEIN :
Well, yes. They were here. . . then they left, didn't
they? They went away.

**Did they go away? And weren't there any arrests?**

MARIUS KLEIN :
Oh yes, there were, all over town.

**Did you see any of them?**

MARIUS KLEIN :
Unfortunately I did.

**Yes. Let's see, when the Jewish laws appeared, I hear you
had an ad put in the newspaper.**

MARIUS KLEIN :
That's right.

**It was an ad in** Le Moniteur?

MARIUS KLEIN :
Well, well. You are well informed, sir. That is
correct. There were four of us, brothers. That's what
I told them when they said we were Jews. My name,
Klein, sounds Jewish, but I am still a Catholic. Well,
of course I was worried; people kept bothering me
about this. So I told them, what with my four
brothers all veterans, that for goodness sake I was
a Frenchman!

**That's it. You made it quite clear to your customers that
you were not a Jew, is that right?**

MARIUS KLEIN :
That's right.

**Why did you do that?**

MARIUS KLEIN :
Well, because it seemed I was thought to be Jewish,
and they were arresting Jews, you see. So I said :
This is not fair. I cannot call myself a Jew if I am
a Catholic. You understand? So then, as you said, I
placed an ad in the paper. Since I had had four
brothers in the war, one who was killed, and the
other three prisoners. . .

77.

**But a great many Jews also had brothers killed during the First World War!**

MARIUS KLEIN:
Listen, I've never been a racist. What difference whether I was Jewish or Moslem, the only thing I knew was this: When a man has done his duty, I consider him to be a Frenchman like me, like all the others.

**That's right.**

MARIUS KLEIN:
Do you see what I mean?

**You did not belong to any of those minorities which the Hitler regime was persecuting. But did you know any Jews, Communists, or Freemasons who were persecuted?**

MARCEL VERDIER, pharmacist in Clermont:
Well, as for Jews, I came to know more Jews than I will ever know again in my life. I had two student helpers working in my pharmacy who were considered evil-minded because they were Jewish. One was the daughter of a Parisian engineer, a remarkable man, and she herself was a remarkable girl, very well brought up. The other girl was the daughter of one of my colleagues at Strasbourg called Hirsch. No one would have anything to do with these two children, they had been banished: the Inspector of Pharmacies had gone to all the pharmacists in town and said, ''You will not give work to those two girls.''

FRENCH NEWSREEL, *speech at French Institute for Jewish Affairs:*
*The film business was to them a golden opportunity: the chance to steal millions. Tannenzaft, known as Nathan, who was French cinema's representative to the world—Oh, unhappy France—has cost the economy almost 700 million francs.*

**Mr. President, did you go to the movies often in those days?**

78.

Paris 1942: All Jews are required to wear this sign of identification.

PIERRE MENDES-FRANCE, former Prime Minister:
Oh yes, I went to the movies quite often. First
because I love movies, but I also had another reason:
I soon discovered that it was a comfortable and
pleasant shelter. You could go at three in the
afternoon, stay for hours and hours in the dark, and
escape any attention. It was really a very good
hiding place.

In many pre-war French movies, there had been
Jewish actors and Jewish directors. Their names
were now erased from the credit titles.

FRENCH NEWSREEL, *in court:*
*Paris. Actualités Mondiales has been able to film part
of the fascinating trial of the Jew Tannenzaft, known
as Bernard Nathan. Our indiscreet presence seems
to make the accused quite uncomfortable. He would*

*prefer more discretion. He raises an objection, but is overruled by the court.*

PIERRE LE CALVEZ, movie theater owner in Clermont: Without applying enormous pressure, the Germans were able to push their movies. There were operettas, movies, the first color films. We saw the first color films, films like *The Golden City*. That wasn't propaganda. But others were out-and-out propaganda. *The Jew Süss*, for instance, was propaganda.

PIERRE MENDES-FRANCE:
Perhaps the most revolting thing is that these movies were not presented as German-made films—which would have been understandable since we had been defeated, since we were under the heel of the Germans anyway—but that they were presented by French authorities as French-made: made on behalf of French organizations, and dubbed, of course, by French actors.

EXCERPT FROM The Jew Süss, *credit titles:*
*The European Cinematographic Alliance presents:*
The Jew Süss, *a film by Veit Harlan de la Terra. The events in this film are based on historical fact.*

PIERRE MENDES-FRANCE:
At the start certain people probably went to this movie like they went to see other German films. Then very quickly you realized that it was a classic propaganda movie, of the most odious and revolting type. There was a sort of boycott then, the spectators went more or less on strike. Even people who were not very keen on the Resistance and who had become used to seeing the usual German movies felt a sort of disgust and refused to have anything to do with this one.

EXCERPT FROM The Jew Süss, *anti-Semitic, "historical" movie:*

[A courtroom in sixteenth-century Würtemberg:]

Judge: *Gentlemen, the criminal record of this Jew does not take into account the shame, miseries, and sufferings endured by our people while under his tyranny. For this reason, I call upon the one of us who has suffered most cruelly of all.*

Storm: *I ask nothing. You are the judges. Judge according to the strictest law.*

Judge: *I beg of you, Storm. No one here has more right than you to judge.*

Storm: *It is not my place. My suffering is too biased. It would be an injustice. But I see here an article of old criminal law which may apply: "If ever a Jew should commit an act of the flesh with a Christian woman, then he shall be publicly hanged from the town gallows, as fair punishment for his crime, and so that his death be a warning to others."*

[At the gallows.]

Prisoner: *Have mercy! I have done no harm! I have always acted on behalf of my master. It is not my fault if your duke has betrayed you! I swear to you that I can make amends, I swear it! Take all my possessions, take all my money, but spare me my life! I am innocent. I am only a poor Jew, spare me my life! I want to live! I want to live!*

[Prisoner is hanged.]

Judge: *The Council of State thus proclaims the will of the people of Würtemberg: All Jews must leave Würtemberg within three days. This applies to the entire country. Decree issued in Stuttgart on the 4th of February, 1738. May our descendents remember it forever. By respecting this decree they will be spared much suffering and much misfortune, and they shall preserve the purity of their blood from the blemishes of this accursed race.*

PIERRE LE CALVEZ, movie theater owner in Clermont: There was a certain audience for *The Jew Süss*: the anti-Semite, first of all—the anti-Semite who felt avenged, if you like, and who enjoyed it; and then there were the collaborators; and then there were people who happened to come in by chance. Eighty percent of the audience went to see it just as they might go to see *Three Argentinians in Paris* or any other similar nonsense being shown at the time on the screen. The German films were not much. No, they really weren't much. They had a lot of French actors in them, because they were making French films in Germany even before the war. La Continentale was a company which made French films. Tino Rossi and all those people used to work for La Continentale.

FRENCH NEWSREEL, *at train station:*
*For the good of art, these screen stars are getting ready to leave for Germany. Here at the Gare de l'Est we recognize: Albert Préjean, Danielle Darrieux, Suzy Delair, Junie Astor, Viviane Romance. Invited by Dr. Karl Fröhlich, President of the German Cinema Corporation in Vienna, Munich, and Berlin.*

Movie stars leaving for Germany, from left to right: Viviane Romance, Danielle Darrieux, Junie Astor, Suzy Delair.

FRENCH NEWSREEL, *General Heydrich's visit to Paris:*
*Paris. The arrival of Monsieur Heydrich, General of the S.S. Chief of Security, Reich representative in Prague. Monsieur Himmler, Chief of the S.S. and of the German police, has asked him to oversee the official inauguration of Monsieur Oberg, Unit*

*General of the S.S. and police in the Occupied*
*Territories, into his new duties. We know that*
*Monsieur Heydrich is president of the International*
*Police Commission, and that France has always been*
*represented in this Commission. The General has*
*seen, while in Paris, Monsieur Bousquet of the police*
*department and Monsieur Hiller, administrative*
*representative. Monsieur Heydrich has also met*
*Monsieur Darquier de Pellepoix, who was recently*
*appointed General Commissioner for Jewish Affairs,*
*as well as Monsieur de Brinon.*

March 1943: Darquier de Pellepoix offers the inauguration
for the Institute for the Study of Jewish Questions.

**What was Paris like in those days?**

CHRISTIAN DE LA MAZIERE, former volunteer in the
French Waffen S.S.:
There were two Parises then, the Paris of people
trying to survive, and the Paris of social life, the

Paris of café society. No doubt about it. Everyone is ashamed to speak about it now. Believe me, Maxim's was full. Le Boeuf sur le Toit was full. The movie industry was in full swing. And I was told that good movies were being made at last because "a certain kind of producer" had gone into exile in the United States. Many directors from that time continue to direct films today, and quite successfully, but they have managed to forget everything they said at the time.

All that made a very lively Paris, a Paris of wild gaiety. Don't worry, there were plenty of very fashionable, very amusing Parisian nights. As I say, only the latest "in" discothèque was missing!


LOUIS GRAVE:
Come along friends. This way, Pierre.

**What happened in this cellar?**

LOUIS GRAVE:
Well in this cellar. . . lots of things took place in this cellar. Practically speaking, the beginning of the Resistance in Auvergne. The evening the first arms

Paris nightclub act.

arrived, we came to this cellar. I remember we sang the "Internationale." We weren't Communists though; it was just that Pétain sang "La Marseillaise," so we had to sing "l'Internationale."

**IN COURTYARD OF THE LYCEE PASCAL.**
MONSIEUR DIONNET, librarian at Lycée Pascal, Clermont:
People came to this flag-raising ceremony against their will, you understand. It was a. . .

**But they came anyway?**

MONSIEUR DIONNET:
Well they had to, in times like that, you begin to realize. . . you understand what people are really like, you know; how fear prevails, with very few exceptions.

**Did they actually run any risk for not attending?**

MONSIEUR DIONNET:
No, but they thought they did.

MONSIEUR DANTON, teacher at Lycée Pascal, Clermont:

In the wine cellar of the Grave brothers.

Listen, I have the distinct impression that there were quite a few young people in our classes who were eager to support de Gaulle. In particular there was the son of a colleague—I can't remember his name . . . and a few others.

**What about the faculty?**

MONSIEUR DANTON :
Well, I can't say about the faculty. They were sympathetic towards these young people, but they had none of the impulsive nature, honestly—none of the vigor you found among the young.

**How do you explain that? What you mention here seems to be true in general.**

MONSIEUR DANTON :
Well, young people are generally much more sincere, and in general more alive. They reflect less about what they do, maybe. Maybe they are also less cautious as a rule. It was nice in a way, their attitude. Don't you think so, Dionnet?

MONSIEUR DIONNET :
They are less scared.

MONSIEUR DANTON :
I had some students in class who were arrested. I can't say precisely how many, not that many, really —the streets were named after them. I'm thinking of Bacaud for instance, whom I had in the sixth grade; the street is in Fontviège. A charming boy, by the way.

**He was in the Resistance?**

MONSIEUR DANTON :
Yes. These people formed a secret network. We didn't know about it. We only found out later. They went on playing the part of schoolboys, but after a time we learned what was going on. Perhaps Dionnet, who was in the Resistance, knew what was happening.

**What was it like for the others? How did the others react when there was suddenly an empty bench one morning in the classroom?**

MONSIEUR DANTON :
Well, it's hard to say. I don't remember that
exactly.

**When a boy's parents were arrested, and the next day the
son was sitting at his bench in class, was there any. . . ?**

MONSIEUR DANTON :
I don't remember.

**You don't remember either?**

MONSIEUR DIONNET :
I don't remember either. I don't know of any specific
instances of that happening.

**But on the walls over there are some specific instances.**

MONSIEUR DIONNET :
Oh, but those are from the First World War, aren't
they?

**From the Second World War too.**

MONSIEUR DIONNET :
Really?

---

FRENCH NEWSREEL, *Pétain visits Clermont-Ferrand:
Clermont-Ferrand welcomes Marshal Pétain with
enthusiasm. The Head of State has come to approve
the constitution of the Regional Union of Farms
and to attend the closing ceremony of the Winter
Crusade for National Welfare. After the ceremony,
the Head of State will receive gifts to the National
Welfare Fund, contributed by farmers who have
come from all corners of the area. A symbolic
ceremony which gives full meaning to the great
crusade of French mutual help. A great day when
the nation has heard its true heartbeat opened up
with hope!*

[Maurice Chevalier sings:]

*J'ai chanté l'amour*    *I sang songs about love,*
*J'ai chanté ya d'la joie*    *I sang songs about happy*
*Sans grande joie*        *days.*
    *pourtant;*    *Even when I was blue*

J'entonnais un petit air
à pleine voix.
L'air fut étouffant.
Désormais quels seront
donc les pauvres mots
Ou les chansons gaies
que pour vous on
invente
Qu'on osera placer
sans risquer trop?
Pour ne pas me tromper
moi voilà ce que je
chante:
tra la la la la la
de ba boum ba boum
avec un ou deux hop la
hop la!
Si vous voulez savoir
Ce que mon coeur pense
ce soir
En chantant comme ça
Tra la la la la:
C'est notre espoir!
En somme l'important
c'était de recommencer
Qu'importe l'expression?
L'essentiel était de
pouvoir dispenser
Du rêve en chansons.
Un poète aurait trouvé
les mots qu'il faut
Qui aurait rime ses voeux
d'espérance.
Moi mon espoir c'est que
le ciel redevienne beau
Et qu'on chante en paix
dans notre vieille
France:
tra la la la la . . .
Si vous voulez savoir
Ce que mon coeur pense
ce soir
En chantant comme ça
Tra la la la la:
C'est notre espoir!

I carried my little tune.


But now I can no longer
find the words
To brighten up your
day,
And so I just say:




tra la la la la la
di ba boom ba boom
with a couple of oupla
oupla's.
If you want to know
what's in my heart
tonight
Sing along with me.
Tra la la la la:
And let's have hope!
The main thing for us
now is to start again
And create dreams with
our songs again.
Maybe a poet could find
the right words, but I
can't,
And so I just say:
Let's hope for a bright
blue sky again
And let's sing together
in dear old France:


tra la la la . . .
If you want to know
what's in my heart
tonight
Sing along with me
Tra la la la la:
And let's have hope!


[End of the First Part.]

At top: German military concert in the park. At bottom: At the iron foundry, the head of Victor Hugo is crushed to produce metal.

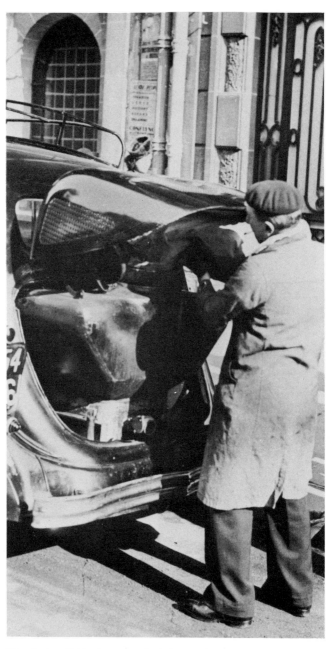

March 10, 1941, the new fuel in Paris: a driver fills his engine with charcoal.

90.

Paris, April 1943: During food shortage, workers cultivating
beans and potatoes on the esplanade of the Invalides.

German soldiers in Paris.

92.

GERMAN NEWSREEL :
*It is early morning on November 11th, 1942, at the
German–French demarcation line: 7:00 A.M. By
order of the Führer, German motorized forces begin
their march through unoccupied France towards the
Mediterranean Coast. In this way Germany responds
to the English-American attack upon French North
Africa and thus prevents the planned enemy landing
upon the coast of southern France.*

ROGER TOUNZE, newspaperman in Clermont :
Well at first we called them Fritzes, then Fridolins,
then Frisés, Frisous. . . "doryphores," and who
knows what else. . . The popular imagination was
very fertile; everyday we had a new name for them.

**Why "doryphores"?**

ROGER TOUNZE:
Because the "doryphore" is a beetle that eats up
potatoes and leaves nothing. Well, when the Germans
passed by they didn't leave anything either.

**No potatoes. . .**

ROGER TOUNZE :
*Especially* no potatoes.

MATHEUS BLEIBINGER, Wehrmacht soldier stationed
in Auvergne :
I still remember a few words from then—civilities,
how to invite girls to go for a walk. "S'il vous plait,
Mademoiselle, voulez-vous promener avec moi?
Bonjour monsieur. Bonne nuit madame."

GERMAN NEWSREEL, *in park:*
*. . . and at noontime, a concert in the park in the
cities of the occupied territories.*

# The Sorrow and the Pity

**Chronicle of a French city under the German occupation.
Second Part: The Choice**

RAPHAEL GEMINIANI, champion cyclist from
Clermont:
In those days there were few bicycle races. In '40,
we had a really dark period—we had to wait till
'41, '42, '43 to see the first races. As a matter of
fact, I started racing in 1943.

**In '43?**

RAPHAEL GEMINIANI:
Yes, in the Dunlop finals. With Bobet as a matter of
fact; we were classmates. You must realize that at
the time cycling was one of the means of
transportation. In fact it was the only one.

During gasoline scarcity, a ''taxi'' stand at the porte de
Vincennes.

**You became a young man at a difficult time. For instance,
girls?**

RAPHAEL GEMINIANI:
Girls?

94.

**Yes, girls—how was it during the occupation?**

RAPHAEL GEMINIANI:
Well, it was a problem, of course. First of all we were
young. . . . The Avenue des Etats-Unis was a solid
mass of people on Sunday or in the evenings when
everyone would take walks up and down the avenue;
that was called "doing the avenue." We walked from
Gaillard to place Jaude, and from place Jaude to
Gaillard, and everyone met.

**Was it annoying for a young man to see a girl arm in arm
with a German?**

RAPHAEL GEMINIANI :
Well yes, of course, it wasn't liked. That was true
everywhere of course, not just in Clermont. A
woman accompanied by a German was disliked
everywhere. Some did go out with the Germans, but
they paid for it during the Liberation. Some paid
quite dearly for going out with the Germans.

In fact there were not too many Germans in
Clermont, because after all it was in the unoccupied
zone.

**But after '42, the Germans were there weren't they?**

RAPHAEL GEMINIANI :
Well, we saw them. . . no, we only saw them when
the Maquis came, but after all, we were not occupied.

**We were told there were very few Germans in Clermont-
Ferrand. Is that true?**

MARCEL VERDIER, pharmacist in Clermont:
I saw too many of them. I used to see them
everywhere. I saw them by day, and when I was
sleeping I saw them in my dreams. They had these
chains around their necks with a sort of medal you
know. I used to see them everywhere. All I saw was
helmets, all I saw was Germans.

**How do you explain that others didn't notice them?**

MARCEL VERDIER :
Well they must have been pretty blind you know
because, my God, I saw them everywhere. . . .

HELMUT TAUSEND, Captain of the Wehrmacht in Clermont:
I was fighting on the Russian front. I was wounded in January '42—my feet were frostbitten and they declared me no longer fit for service in the East. That's why I was sent back to France in '42. Of course, for a regular officer, it was a little humiliating to be in France, because for us the victory was being won on the Eastern Front.

**Yes, though it was not won .**

HELMUT TAUSEND:
No, unfortunately not, but we could not predict that at the time. My commanding officer understood my reservations. He told me: ''My dear Tausend, just play the fool, and you'll soon be transferred back to us.'' But that was not to be, and I stayed on in Clermont until the end of the war.

**Why? You didn't know how to play the fool?**

HELMUT TAUSEND:
No, I must say I didn't have much of a gift for it. Everything was still very quiet in Clermont at the end of '42. Our work was to train troops, especially in anti-guerilla operations. People in Clermont liked us very much: our relations were good, and as far as they were concerned, there was no distinction between Frenchmen and Germans. We used to live in a hotel in Royat. I think I still have some photos. ...

MONSIEUR MIOCHE, owner of hotel in Royat, outside Clermont:
So I had to endure them. As customers go, there's nothing to reproach them for.

**It's interesting you should say you ''had to endure them.'' Were they difficult to endure?**

MONSIEUR MIOCHE :
Well they stopped me from doing my work, you know what I mean. I could have put up a few regular customers instead. . . because you see the Germans did not pay me. . . .

HELMUT TAUSEND :
As far as *we* were concerned, we could buy anything
at all : cheese, ham, sausage. You could buy anything
on the black market.

**Did you feel that those people who had some contact with
you—the shopkeepers, the hotel owners—did those sort of
people make themselves unpopular somehow with their
countrymen for having contact with you?**

HELMUT TAUSEND :
Oh no, not in '42 anyway. Things started to become
more difficult later on when the so-called
"resistance" began. I think I still have a photo of
that period. Beginning of '43, on the other hand, we
had to surround ourselves with barbed wire !

For example : in broad daylight hand grenades were
thrown at one company of our soldiers while they
were marching to the movie theater—to one of those
theaters reserved for our troops. I don't know
whether those hand grenades were thrown from the
roof tops or what. In any case, eight were killed
and forty were injured.

June 1940: Movie theater for German soldiers on the Champs
Elysées.

PIERRE LE CALVEZ, movie theater owner in
Clermont:
The show began at six o'clock. It was about five
o'clock and the soldiers were marching through town
in formation, protected by armed sentries. They were
not armed themselves, but the sentries around them
were. So terrorists threw bombs down from on top
of the city walls: the wounded soldiers fell, the
ambulances arrived, and the show went on. That's
when those terrible reprisals took place; they set
fire to the whole upper part of Clermont looking
for people. They picked up an enormous number of
young people.

Burning of the village of Manlay by the Wehrmacht as
reprisal for acts of Resistance saboteurs.

HELMUT TAUSEND:
So obviously this forced us to take strong counter
measures. The partisans themselves, of course, the
partisans had vanished.

98.

Do you know that on that occasion many people were
arrested at random on the place Jaude, many young men in
particular, who were then deported to Germany?

HELMUT TAUSEND :
No, I knew nothing of the kind. I only knew that in
Clermont there was a Gestapo unit which terrified
the French. People used to say. . . but after all, you
must admit that they were there to protect us.

━━━━━━━━━━━━━━━━━━━━━━━━━━━━━━━━━━━━━━━━━━━━━━━━━━━━━━━━━━━━━━━━━

MONSIEUR MIOCHE, owner of hotel in Royat, outside
Clermont :
You know, the Germans you'd speak to in these
instances always told you the same story : if only the
French and the Germans would unite, that would be
the solution. They would say that everywhere, they
were convinced of it. I really don't know. . . .

**Perhaps they meant it?**

MONSIEUR MIOCHE :
Perhaps. They were even a bit too nice. They knew
they weren't liked, so they overdid it. In streetcars,
for instance, they almost always offered their seats
to older people.

**How did they manage with women for instance?**

MONSIEUR MIOCHE :
Well, one night. . . talking about women. . . you
know Madame Mioche was very strict about it. One
time some men came in after midnight with two
girls. Madame Mioche wouldn't let the girls in. When
they insisted, she went to wake up the captain. When
the captain came down, he supported Madame
Mioche.

**They must not have been very happy. . . .**

MONSIEUR MIOCHE :
Well, they weren't happy, but you know what a
captain is, he's discipline first and above all, right ?
So, Madame Mioche was happy.

**She was, was she?**

MONSIEUR MIOCHE:
Of course, but she was afraid that they'd be allowed in anyway, so she told them: "This is not a house of..."

**A house of ill repute...**

MONSIEUR MIOCHE:
Of course. And so the next day they requisitioned a house across the way, and solved the problem that way.

HELMUT TAUSEND, Captain of the Wehrmacht in Clermont:
As always in time of war when soldiers are far from their home, brothels were set up. And in Clermont there were quite a few because in daylight, in the streets, the girls of Clermont wouldn't even look at us. . . .

**And when it was neither daylight nor in the streets?**

HELMUT TAUSEND:
Well at night, well it's a fact I must say—they were a great deal more friendly. . . .

Things got worse when the Michelin plant was bombed. You know, the famous tire-manufacturing plant—it was working for us, of course. The Americans didn't aim very accurately and the bombs fell all over the place. . . . Well, people resented us for bringing that on them. But I think by the end of '42, beginning of '43, the Resistance had already spread pretty much everywhere.

----

**Were you disturbed that British pilots were bombing France?**

LOUIS GRAVE, farmer near Clermont:
They weren't bombing people, they were bombing factories working for the Germans, that's all. We were at war, we were allies, we were at war against the Germans—we had joined the Resistance, after all. I, for instance, had signed up in London. I had registered there, I had a number in London. It was number 61055; I still remember it.

Flight Sergeant Evans.

FLIGHT SERGEANT EVANS, RAF Pilot shot down in
Auvergne:
The last time I actually flew in one of these was way
back in May, 1944, when we were shot down, but I
had been in one of them since then.

**How long is it now since you were shot down?**

FLIGHT SERGEANT EVANS:
May 1944. Almost twenty-five years to the day.

**You have more difficulty getting into this contraption now
than—**

FLIGHT SERGEANT EVANS:
I've become a bit fatter since those days, I must have
put on at least a couple of stone since 1944, yes. . . .

**You don't look much like a Frenchman.**

FLIGHT SERGEANT EVANS:
No, that's true.

**Did you have that same moustache?**

FLIGHT SERGEANT EVANS:
No this is the point, I *did* have a moustache. . . But
when I got shot down. . . I was advised that there's
not many gingerheaded, moustached Frenchmen
about. And they asked me to shave it off. Which I
did. And they supplied me with a French
demobilization suit—not exactly Carnaby Row style,
or even Savile Row but nevertheless it served its
purpose—and a beret. And of course we had flying
boots that we cut the tops off to form shoes. . .

**Did you find the French population helpful?**

FLIGHT SERGEANT EVANS:
I would say certainly most helpful. I'd say people
were willing to give up their lives for you, because
they knew that if they were caught by the Germans,
that they were shot without any form of trial
whatsoever. People were helping me, a Monsieur
Sauçay. . . I didn't realize that cigarettes were so
short in France. As was the case in England we
could have as many as we wanted. But he gave me
Gauloises, twenty, virtually twenty a day, which I
smoked and just asked for more. What I didn't
realize and I only found out months later, that
in the evening when I was in bed he was going
around emptying the ashtrays, gathering up my
stub-ends, my cigarette ends, and making them into
cigarettes himself.

LOUIS GRAVE:
We used to go into the woods over there, to my
father's house, that's where the weapons were
hidden, and that's where we cleaned them. . . .

**And the weapons caches?**

ALEXIS GRAVE:
Some were in the woods there and some were further
out in the vineyards, in those woods up there. There
must still be some there.

102.

**How did you manage? Since it was a small town, people must have suspected something after awhile. How did the others—those who weren't in the Resistance—what did they do?**

LOUIS GRAVE:
Well, they kept quiet.

**They kept quiet, really?**

LOUIS GRAVE:
Pétain's police came and they put me in jail at Clermont. Then I was sent to the jailhouse at Mélisse. I stayed there for one day, then I was sent to the jailhouse at ''Deux Bis.'' I was sent up twice on the same day, and the next day I was sent up five times.

**Were you tortured? Beaten?**

LOUIS GRAVE:
Well they didn't hand out lollipops you know. They had found eleven—no, twelve—parachutes in my house, and they wanted to know where they came from. They wanted to know everything, these gentlemen.

**Did they ever get what they were after?**

LOUIS GRAVE:
No they didn't. . . .
Well we were freed—I mean they put us out on the roads. For three days we were led along the roads, until they left us in a little village called Itsdorf—I remember it well, I'll always remember Saxony, over there near the Elbe.

**Did you have any pictures of yourself at the time?**

LOUIS GRAVE:
Oh no, I was much too ugly. I didn't want any pictures taken.

**Why? How much did you weigh?**

LOUIS GRAVE:
Ninety-two pounds.

**And you didn't want any photographs taken?**

LOUIS GRAVE:
No. I didn't. There was no point in anyone seeing
me like this, I thought.

**You wanted to wait until you were. . .**

LOUIS GRAVE:
That's it. . .

**More handsome!**

LOUIS GRAVE:
Yes, I saw a lot of misery. I saw a convoy of
prisoners coming in from Hungary—I think it was
Hungary, anyway—there were fifty thousand of
them. Not one of them. . . . Well, I remember I was
sent out to take them soup, it was near the movie
theater in Buchenwald—there was even a movie
theater in Buchenwald, there was everything, even
a brothel, and that's the truth! So we brought them
the soup, and they jumped at it—fifty thousand of
them, they jumped on that soup—they overturned
the things, they got down on their knees in the middle
of the mud. There was about a foot and a half of
mud, well maybe not a foot and a half, but almost a
foot of mud anyway. Well, they ate the soup right
there in the mud, the poor guys. . . . And four days
later they were all wiped out.

And that's how things were at Buchenwald.

---

**Did you notice much difference between classes in French
society at the time?**

DENIS RAKE, British secret agent in occupied France:
Yes indeed. I would say the greatest help I received
came from railroad workers and Communists. French
workers were terrific, they would do anything, they
would give you their last penny if you had no
money. I stayed with a family who had only one room
and a kitchen and I slept in the kitchen. This was in
Juvisy, close to Paris, so it was a very dangerous
place then. They lent me dungarees to wear because
I had to walk around and draw the network of trains
we were planning to bomb. I was a radio operator
and this was not quite my job, but to make things
go faster I always helped out.

Denis Rake.

**You speak about workers. How about the French middle
class, what were they doing?**

DENIS RAKE:
The middle class was very neutral. I must say they
didn't help me very much. I found working people
really wonderful—waiters, salesgirls and so on. I
had mailboxes in the big department stores, and I
don't know whether all these people knew what they
were doing, since we didn't explain to them the
danger involved in all this. I always found everything I needed through workers. But the middle
class was scared. Of course they had more to lose,
and I think in life that one often takes into account
what one has to lose. As far as I was concerned, I
had nothing to lose—I had no relatives, I wasn't
married. That's why I did that kind of work—
what difference did it make after all?

MAURICE BUCKMASTER, former Chief, British underground:

Denis Rake was a boy—I say a boy—although he is older than I am—who had faith, a sense of patriotism and a very deep sense of duty. The reason he was so courageous was that he was basically a shy man, and he hated firearms. We needed such people, because they were the ones who had the courage to conquer their fears.

DENIS RAKE :

I think deep down what I wanted to do was to be able to display the same kind of courage my friends who had become flyers had. Being a homosexual, one of my strongest fears was lacking the courage to do certain things.

**You had somehow adopted other people's prejudices, so you thought that, given your tendencies, you'd be less courageous than others, is that it?**

DENIS RAKE :

Yes I did. I certainly thought so.

**Do you think being a man of the theater predisposed you for these underground activities?**

DENIS RAKE :

Very much so. I used to sing as a transvestite. So in Paris I worked at the Grand Ecart for three months, then at the Cave Caucasienne for a good while.

**Did you have an affair during that time?**

DENIS RAKE :

Yes I did form a great friendship with a German officer. It started because I had no papers and I went to a nightclub where I met someone I knew who introduced me to this man who was able to get me the papers. But this acquaintance turned to great friendship. Like all these friendships do, it is a question of speed, and he invited me to stay with him and I stayed for about four or five months until I found that I was thinking that I was letting him down in this double game business, and I was always afraid that if I should confess to him the truth it should put him in an awkward position, so I decided to . . .

106.

**He didn't know you were English?**

DENIS RAKE :
No, he thought I was Belgian. So I decided to ask
for a recall. It was just my affection became so
deep. . . .

**Yes, but you were fighting the Germans.**

DENIS RAKE :
Yes and I was also fighting against him, wasn't I
really?

**All sorts of conflicts. . .**

DENIS RAKE :
Yes. He was transferred to a regiment which went
to Russia.

**What happened to him in Russia?**

DENIS RAKE :
I believe he was killed. I asked here in England, our
headquarters, and they found out for me.

**They did that as a favor to you?**

DENIS RAKE :
Yes, I suppose so, they were always very good to me.

MAURICE BUCKMASTER :
We put together a group and armed them with
weapons delivered by parachute from London. They
were to block the passage of German troops. We sent
them Denis Rake as a radio operator. Like any other
underground unit, the "Mont Mouchez" unit was
composed of people who refused to go into the STO,
compulsory labor in Germany, and grouped together
in Auvergne. We didn't know, of course, that on the
night Denis Rake arrived in France, the Germans
had attacked en masse—and that Denis Rake would
land right in the middle of the battle. It seems he
spent the night in a tree, emerging the next day to
send us the message that he had arrived at an
inopportune moment, but that everything was all
right. He was working in the district being organized
around Gaspar. . . .

EMILE COULAUDON, called GASPAR, former leader of
the Auvergne maquis:
What I am really proud of, you might say, is that
old pseudonym Gaspar—after all, my old friends,
like the ones you just saw, wouldn't dream of calling
me "Monsieur Coulaudon." My name Coulaudon is
well-known in my profession of course, but that's a
different story altogether.

Coulaudon's the name of your normal, everyday life,
thirty years later?

EMILE COULAUDON, called GASPAR:
That's right.

MAURICE BUCKMASTER:
And then we were supposed to find this big Maquis
division led by a certain "Gaspar," in Mont
Mouchez. He had a good battle going—a very
brilliant man, really a wonderful man, but he was
hungry—hungry for glory, hungry for everything.

We felt that Gaspar inspired confidence, affection,
even love in his people, in the patriots around him.
There's no doubt he was a great leader.

**WITH GASPAR AND A GATHERING OF RESISTERS**

EMILE COULAUDON, called GASPAR:
So here is the village where the Resistance of
Auvergne first began—this is where the first unit
was formed. Look, a dog coming to meet us. In those
days we had a dog who we nicknamed "de Gaulle."
He always stayed near us. he never left us for two
winters. . . .

What is that monument?

EMILE COULAUDON, called GASPAR:
It's the monument to our comrades who were killed.
The day the Germans surrounded the village here,
we were unable to get back in because there was too
much snow. We were all out on missions—all except
for four young kids whom we'd left behind because
they were still recuperating from wounds. . . and
these four young kids were caught in the nest by
the Germans. They came early in the morning, along
the railroad tracks—it was snowing and there was
less snow along the railroad tracks. They surrounded
the hamlet, and they approached our cottage,

thinking they'd get all of us. But there were only
these four young kids, twenty years old. One of them
came out barefoot in the snow and fought back—a
nineteen-year-old guy from the village of Volvic who
we used to call Milavon—and he used a machine gun
against them but there were too many of them and
they killed him. The Germans left him lying there
on the snow, and he died immediately. The second
kid was caught with his hands up, he didn't have
even the time to get out of bed. And then there were
two young ones left. One had hid himself in a box
he was so small. Nineteen years old. And what was
the name of the kid who was captured here, Tarzan?

MAN STANDING NEARBY:
Half-Ounce.

EMILE COULAUDON, called GASPAR:
Half-Ounce or Four Pounds.
That is what he weighed with no clothes on. And so
they captured him too.

The thing which amazes me most when I talk to
people who I know very well supported Pétain is. . .
they all tell me how they did their share for the
Resistance. They've all done one thing or another,
there's always something they can think of. . .
Sometimes it's quite incredible: ''Well if you only
knew, Monsieur Gaspar, if I told you what I did
. . .'' And so I say: out with it, come on, tell me, tell
me all about it.

I don't want get angry over it. My job is to sell
TV and radios and I want to sell those TV's and
radios, and I'm not paid by my company to get into
political arguments or to split people apart, so I
have to listen to these fairy tales without wincing.
Sometimes they've got tears in their eyes when they
tell you: ''See this drawer here?''

And then he calls his wife out: ''Come here, is it
true or isn't it that I kept a gun right here?'' And
his wife says: ''Oh yes, it used to frighten me a lot
you know. But as my husband used to say: 'It'll
be there when they come, when they come we'll do
what has to be done.' Only they never did what
had to be done.

EMILE COULAUDON, called GASPAR:
Let me say right off that I was only a
non-commissioned officer in the French army. I see
what you're thinking, that I climbed the ladder

109.

awfully quickly maybe. But what was I supposed to do? It was there. . . . One of my friends was referring to this just a minute ago in the car. He was saying: ''But you never had much schooling did you?''

Well that's true, I didn't. But as the former mayor of Combronde, my friend Monsieur Leiris, used to tell me: maybe it's true that I got my diploma from the ''school of crime,'' but if so, it is because the school of crime was the only school where one could learn how to fight against the murderers of our comrades.

Resistance handbill: ''Be Quiet. Enemy ears are listening.''

MONSIEUR LEIRIS, former Mayor of Combronde, resister:

Also, what you mustn't forget is that de Gaulle sent an order from London to all French officers— who were sitting smugly at home in their slippers —ordering them to join the Maquis. If they had really done that, then maybe some of the mistakes could have been avoided, the mistakes—and there *were* mistakes after all—of the Resistance made by those kids who were hiding in the woods rather than joining up with the Germans, rather than going to work in Germany for the Germans, those kids who were *one hundred percent* patriotic, who got themselves killed on every road in France. Maybe if they'd been led by French officers who were toasting their toes at home while the Republic paid for it, dearly. . . .

[Voices objecting.]

MONSIEUR LEIRIS:
Don't say it's not true. . . I know them, I know a lot of them. . . .

EMILE COULAUDON, called GASPAR:
But that's just it. . . .

MONSIEUR LEIRIS:
And lots of them stayed quietly at home: "Oh, what do I know. . ." And I'd ask them then: "Dear boy, why didn't you do like the rest of us?" "Well," they answered, "I didn't know where to go to join the Resistance. I didn't know." Well *I* knew! I knew, and I'm just a poor bastard from around here. But the others, they didn't know!

EMILE COULAUDON, called GASPAR [to others]:
If we had it all over to do again, would you appoint me colonel again, or would you instead make me sergeant or adjutant for example?

**If I understand correctly, Colonel Gaspar is asking you twenty-five years afterwards whether you are willing to give him a vote of confidence again?**

AN OLD MAN:
Certainly. It's thanks to people like him that we were able to do something. Not thanks to the smug ones who stayed at home.

Gaspar.

EMILE COULAUDON, called GASPAR:
Don't think I want a plebiscite now!

He's mixing everything up. I start talking politics
and he says: no mixing wines!... But what I wanted
to hear you say—that there is some Neo-Nazism in
the world which is gradually appearing—and that's
why I thought it fair and natural that we should
take part in these interviews. We used to say "nix"
to talking about it, because we thought—and we still
do—that it shouldn't all be stirred up... a little like
the veterans of Verdun who were heroes but who
become a little silly in the long run, and people
said, "There he goes, telling his life-story again."
I believe that there is a risk in Nazism re-appearing
in the world, or something like Nazism with a
different name.

MONSIEUR LEIRIS:
There is one thing too often forgotten. The Germans,

112.

the Nazis, it's all very well to talk about them, but what about the French? Are any of them better than the Nazis?

EMILE COULAUDON, called GASPAR:
Stop it.

MONSIEUR LEIRIS:
*I* personally had a sixty-year-old woman shot—she'd sold me to the Gestapo for money. For money, me and my son too, to have us both shot.

EMILE COULAUDON, called GASPAR:
Either in Auvergne, where we exposed ourselves maybe unwisely, or in Brittany—or in the Vercors, or anywhere—anyone who *really* wanted to find a branch of the Resistance to join didn't have much difficulty in finding one. If he really wanted to fight, understand, or just to act in clandestine way, without necessarily becoming a fighter himself.

MONSIEUR LEIRIS:
Our first aim was to try to create a certain psychological climate around the Germans, to keep them in partial terror all the time, cutting telegraph wires and waiting for the Allies to land so we could blow up everything. The aim wasn't to kill Germans. What was the point in killing ten, fifty, a hundred Germans I ask you? No, really, our aim was to prevent them from. . .

EMILE COULAUDON, called GASPAR:
Maybe we should add something to what you're saying. We never pretended to be an army facing another army, and yet. . . and yet, because of the enthusiasm which kept growing we did end up with an army of some ten thousand armed men.

HELMUT TAUSEND, Captain of the Wehrmacht in Clermont:
Take this, for instance. A platoon of ours was walking on the outskirts of Clermont-Ferrand, they were passing a group of workers, some twenty or so in all, digging potatoes. Suddenly, these workers throw down their tools, grab for rifles, and shoot down fourteen of our men in a second. You call that "partisan" resistance? I don't. Partisans for me are

men that can be identified, men who wear a special
arm band or a cap, something with which to
recognize them. What happened in that potato field
was murder. That's what I call it. With these sort
of things happening, well, you've got to admit we had
to take harsh measures. I'd go so far as to say it
was our duty as officers, to demand such security
measures for our troops.

**AN EVENING WITH THE GRAVE FAMILY, APRIL, 1969.**

[Louis and Alexis Grave, Madame Grave, Roger
Tounze and several other men are present.]

LOUIS GRAVE:
After we had been liberated, I had to guard some
German prisoners, but I never hurt them, I never
told them off. First, because if I'd done to them what
they'd done to me I'd have put myself into exactly
the same category, and I didn't want to put myself
into that category.

All those old Germans were veterans of the First
World War, old ones from the *Schupo*, you know,
the green police. . . .

What could we do to them? They'd done us no harm.
The ones who had had escaped—they weren't there
any more. But these old ones from the *Schupo*, we
couldn't. . . they hadn't done us any harm. . . .
I remember one of them who broke his rifle. He'd
given me an apple after we'd been on the road,
marching, in ranks, for three days. He was marching
beside me and slipped me an apple. What was I
supposed to do to that man? We had been given one
loaf of bread in the morning, for all twenty two of
us, for the whole walk. . . and we were liberated at
three that afternoon.

**Do you think that, to be a resister, you needed some sort
of political background?**

LOUIS GRAVE:
No.

**Take yourself for instance, did you have any?**

LOUIS GRAVE:
Well, my family's always been on the left and I've
always been on the left—not the extreme left but the
left.

114.

**Do you mean Socialist?**

LOUIS GRAVE:
Socialist. The French Socialist Party. I still am, I
haven't changed, and I'm proud of it—though some
of the old people in the party maybe they're a little
like me, they're a little old. Why do they always
shove old people into the heads of government,
eighty-year-olds and the like? They should be fed to
the pigs!

**There is a myth that some farmers in France became rich
during the war.**

MADAME GRAVE:
Some did, some did. . .

ALEXIS GRAVE:
Some did, yes. . .

LOUIS GRAVE:
Well, today sometimes I say to myself,"by God, if
only you had dealt in the black market—now you'd
be rich and everyone would pay you their respects."
As it is, I stuck with the Resistance so they think
I'm an idiot.

ALEXIS GRAVE:
That's how it goes.

**And today, do you think that having been in the
Resistance gives you a bad or a good reputation with other
people?**

LOUIS GRAVE:
Well, I think it's always given us a bad reputation,
since at the time they used to call us terrorists,
bandits. . . Bandits, anything. And you know the
word stuck with some people. . . .

ALEXIS GRAVE:
And after the war they called us profiteers. . . .

LOUIS GRAVE:
They said we took advantage of the supplies flown
in, that we had received parachute drops. . . .

MADAME GRAVE:
There *were* some in the Resistance—who called

**115.**

themselves resisters—who took advantage of that fact to loot and steal. They took advantage of the moment!

**Weren't there two ways of resisting, either by being anti-German, or by being anti-Nazi?**

At the Grave household: at left, Roger Tounze and Madame Grave.

ROGER TOUNZE:
Anti-German and anti-Nazi: my dear friend, for us it was the same thing. For a while I thought like you that a distinction should be made between the German people and the Nazis. Then when I was taken prisoner and beaten with sticks and starved— well, I'm sorry, but my reaction was that of a starving man: I just lumped them all in the same bag.

LOUIS GRAVE:
I realized that certain Germans weren't Nazis, but those who weren't Nazis were in concentration camps. You mustn't forget that concentration camps began in Germany in 1933.

ROGER TOUNZE:
We used to say that all Germans were Nazis, that there were no Communists left in Germany, that they were all in concentration camps. So, since they

116.

were in concentration camps, I didn't feel that I was
hurting a Communist when I came face to face with
a German.

**There weren't any Communists in Wehrmacht uniform?**

ROGER TOUNZE:
There shouldn't have been, and even if there were
some, I wasn't going to ask, especially since I don't
speak German.

A SECOND OLD MAN:
The Germans who fought against the Auvergne
maquis were all Nazis.

FIRST OLD MAN:
They were all S.S. troops.

THE SECOND OLD MAN:
All of them Nazis or S.S.—but *super* Nazi! That's
all there was!

**Did you kill any Germans?**

LOUIS GRAVE:
Well, of course, but I didn't see them. After all,
when you're in action behind a machine gun, you
don't know where your bullets are landing.

**What about "bad Frenchmen"?**

ROGER TOUNZE:
Well, I knew many "bad Frenchmen," but
personally I never killed any.

**And you?**

FIRST OLD MAN:
Well no, neither did I.

---

EMMANUEL D'ASTIER DE LA VIGERIE, former Secretary
of State, resister:
I was already a black sheep... in my social class...
since I had married an American divorcee, who was
incidentally a Roosevelt. I had done many things:
I had smoked opium, I had written scandalous
editorials all over the place, and so I was considered
a black sheep, and an unsuccessful black sheep at

that! And when black sheep like that become successful, they're still at odds with society. Yet despite my weakness for Communists, my family still, on the day I became a minister in the Liberation Government, reclaimed me! And that's the main thing.

What did I get out of the Resistance? The most important thing, outside a certain dignity, was—and I'll say it again and again—that it is the only period in my life when I lived in a truly classless society.

MARCEL FOUCHE-DEGLIAME, former editor of *Combat*, Resistance newspaper:
The problems of everyday life no longer existed; we were very free. . .

EMMANUEL D'ASTIER:
I'm going to say something nasty about my friends and myself: I think you could only have joined the Resistance if you were maladjusted.

MARCEL FOUCHE-DEGLIAME:
Free in the sense that, being outside organized society, all of society's objectives did not affect us very much, it simply didn't matter anymore.

EMMANUEL D'ASTIER:
It's impossible to imagine a government minister, or a colonel, or an executive becoming a real partisan, a resister; if they're successful in their lives, then they'll be equally successful in dealing with Germans or Englishmen or Russians. But for all of us "failures"—and I was a failure—well, we had the kind of Quixotic feelings that failures can always have.

GEORGES BIDAULT, former President of the National Resistance Council:
Some people resist naturally, in other words they are stubborn. And others, on the contrary, try to adapt to circumstances and make the best of it. So, if you resist everything and anything, well it's obvious that you're overdoing it; and if you adjust to everything, it's obvious you're not being truthful.

EMMANUEL D'ASTIER:
There were six of us—a gas company employee, a

pimp, a bus driver, a butcher from Quipavas, and a
few others like that. And there on the piers of
Port-Vendres, I found men who had fled like all
the rest, like me, men who were now saying: what
can we do? And I said: "Well, why not try
resistance?" I went down the coast, and near
Saint-Jean-de-Luz, I found an English ship which
had orders not to take Frenchmen—as a matter of
fact, it was supposed to take the Polish division back
to London. So I said: "Well, why not go to Navy
headquarters where they'll be up to something."
So I arrived at my division headquarters in
Collioure. The officers were installed in a brothel
since there wasn't room anywhere else: they had
kicked out the poor girls who were there and settled
themselves in their stead. But they told me: "What's
this story about 'resisting'? You're crazy!" So I had
myself discharged. I went to Marseilles with some
other men, and I realized there that we had to do
something within France. . . there was no longer any
question of leaving the country.

JACQUES DUCLOS, Communist Party Chief during
occupation:
As is known, at that time we served as a magnetic
pole for many patriots who recognized in us a
determined core—because, after all, we were
fighters, whereas there were a lot of talkers. There
were a lot of drawingroom resisters you know. We
weren't drawingroom heroes: we were fighters. An
amazing thing happened: a Communist militant, who
perhaps didn't quite realize the greatness of his
gesture, a metal worker named Jean-Pierre Timbaud,
shouted, just as he was about to be shot by the Nazis
at Châteaubriant: "Long live the German
Communist party!" You understand. . .

**Why are you an anti-Communist, Colonel?**

COLONEL R. DU JONCHAY, former resister, of
monarchist leanings:
Well. . . because I am a Catholic, that's my main
reason. I realize that they took part in the Resistance,
but I also realize that. . . they did it for the most
part to defend Russia—Communist Russia, their
mother country. . .

Yes, their mother country. . .

COLONEL R. DU JONCHAY :
. . . Even though they have no country, I mean they say they're international, but still, Russia is the country which upholds this ideal.

JACQUES DUCLOS :
The big argument was the following : should we keep our army stored away on the shelf, or should we keep it fighting and growing stronger day by day ?

With such differences between your opinions and theirs, how did you manage to bring any sense of national unity to the Resistance?

COLONEL R. DU JONCHAY :
I did it very poorly. As regional leader for Limoges, I never once contacted the Communists. Not once.

Marcel Fouché-Degliame

**But you were instructed to do so?**

COLONEL R. DU JONCHAY:
Yes, I had been ordered to.

**Those orders came from London?**

COLONEL R. DU JONCHAY:
Yes.

MARCEL FOUCHE-DEGLIAME:
In general, the establishment considered us extremely
dangerous individuals. Really they thought we were
going to send France through fire and blood with
ill-considered actions. . . .

COLONEL R. DU JONCHAY:
. . . Yes, we were surprised by London's insistence
on forming a united front within the Resistance
movements. . . . We thought it was dangerous to arm
the Communists, since there were some very
questionable elements in their ranks and we thought
there would be trouble later, at the time of the
Liberation.

**You were, I believe, in charge of the terrorist groups, those
who had to commit the killings? Did you yourself
participate in these?**

MARCEL FOUCHE-DEGLIAME:
I myself carried out some sabotage, but never any
killings. I never deliberately killed a German in the
street.

**But you would have?**

MARCEL FOUCHE-DEGLIAME:
I would have if I had been asked to, but that wasn't
my work. . . .

**Questionable elements. You say the Communists were full
of questionable elements. . . .**

COLONEL R. DU JONCHAY:
They recruited among. . . convicts, for instance.

JACQUES DUCLOS:
And that's why, for example, we glorified the gesture
of Pierre George, "Colonel Fabien," who killed a
German at the métro Barbès. We had to get people
used to the idea of fighting. There were two ways
of looking at things then: either go underground—
since lists of executed hostages were posted along
the streets of Paris—or resign yourself to do nothing
and fall into despair; or else fight.

COLONEL R. DU JONCHAY:
The army gave the order to stand by and wait and
these Communists were in favor of immediate
guerilla action: assassinations, sabotages, etc. You
see, they were disobeying the orders from London.

Resistance partisans of the Forces Francaises de l'Intérieur
(FFI) preparing to sabotage railroad tracks.

122.

JACQUES DUCLOS:
We said that orders like that should not be obeyed,
and we quoted one of de Gaulle's catch-phrases, even
if we turned it somewhat against him. We said: "The
National insurrection is inseparable from the
liberation."

MARCEL FOUCHE-DEGLIAME:
Resistance is permanent guerilla warfare. Three guys
intercepting a German convoy on a road, throwing
three grenades, firing their machine guns, and
disappearing into the countryside. And that was the
only way, not only for training fighters, but for
keeping them.

Anti-American propaganda in Paris: FDR as the bombing
murderer of French civilians.

Page opposite:
Anti-Resistance poster: "Here's the proof! If some Frenchmen pillage, steal, sabotage, and kill . . . It is always foreigners who command them! It is always jobless and professional criminals who carry out the orders! It is always the Jews who inspire them! They are **THE ARMY OF CRIME** against France! Banditry is not the expression of wounded patriotism, it is a foreign plot against the life of Frenchmen and the sovereignty of France. It is the anti-France conspiracy! It is the world dream of Jewish sadism . . . Let us strangle it before it strangles us, our wives, and our children!"

# A bas les Affameurs !

**PEUPLE DE PARIS !**
LES DENREES ARRIVENT MAL.
LES TIENS SOUFFRENT.

# A qui la Faute ?

Le Gouvernement s'emploie à ravitailler les villes tant bien que mal, mais

**qui coupe les ponts ?**
**qui fait dérailler les trains ?**
**qui bombarde les gares ?**
**qui mitraille sur les routes les camions de farine ?**
**qui incendie les récoltes et anéantit le bétail ?**

**Les ANGLAIS - Les AMERICAINS - Les TERRORISTES**

*QUI DONNE L'ORDRE DE VOUS AFFAMER ?*

Le 10 Juin à 21 h. 45 l'ex-député communiste WALDECK-ROCHET déclarait au micro de RADIO-LONDRES :

"Plus une locomotive, plus un wagon ne doivent être en état "de rouler. Plus une voie de chemin de fer ne doit subsister; les "camions doivent être sabotés. Pas un grain de blé, pas un "gramme de viande ne doit parvenir à Paris. Préparez la grève "dans les campagnes pour affamer les villes et faciliter par la "famine la grève générale."

Parce que la guerre civile voulue par Londres et Moscou n'a pas eu lieu, vos bourreaux veulent vous jeter dans LA REVOLUTION DU DESESPOIR.

**Contre les affameurs assassins, faites le front de l'ordre français.**

LA FEDERATION REGIONALE DE L'ILE-DE-FRANCE
DE LA MILICE FRANÇAISE

July, 1944, poster of the French Militia: "Down With Those Who Starve You! . . . Who cuts the bridges? Who derails the trains? Who bombs the train stations? . . . The English, the Americans, the Terrorists. Who gave the order to starve you? . . . the former Communist deputy Waldeck-Rochet . . . Against those who starve and murder, keep up the front of French Order!"

124.

# Voici la preuve

Si des Français pillent, volent, sabotent et tuent...

**Ce sont toujours des étrangers qui les commandent.**

**Ce sont toujours des chômeurs et des criminels professionnels qui exécutent.**

**Ce sont toujours des juifs qui les inspirent.**

C'est

# L'ARMÉE DU CRIME

## contre la France

Le Banditisme n'est pas l'expression du Patriotisme blessé, c'est le complot étranger contre la vie des Français et contre la souveraineté de la France.

C'EST LE COMPLOT DE L'ANTI-FRANCE!...

C'EST LE RÊVE MONDIAL DU SADISME JUIF...

**ÉTRANGLONS-LE AVANT QU'IL NOUS ÉTRANGLE NOUS, NOS FEMMES ET NOS ENFANTS !**

---

Do you think France is marked today, or to some extent even determined, by what happened to it during the war, I mean between '39 and '44?

EMMANUEL D'ASTIER DE LA VIGERIE, former Secretary of State, resister:

Certainly, certainly. De Gaulle started off his whole political career by pretending to play on the trust of the people. It was a rather peculiar thing. I think that if in 1940 a referendum had been held, that 90 percent of the French people would have voted for Pétain, and for a mild German occupation. So de Gaulle was completely against the trend of historical currents.

Anti-Gaullist propaganda: "The true face of the Free French: the Microphone General, 'protector' of the Jews!"

ENGLISH NEWSREEL, *De Gaulle's broadcast to the nation, June 18, 1940:*
*The Free French do not accept this defeat. The Free French do not consent to an arrangement whereby, under the pretext of keeping order and harmony in Europe, their country be used as a base for the enemy from which to attack other countries fighting for the same ideal. . . .*

EMMANUEL D'ASTIER DE LA VIGERIE :
. . . until the day I said: "I want to see General de Gaulle myself!" I was very poorly received. I found myself facing a man who astounded me: here he was already, plainly and simply the king of France.

126.

June 18, 1940: de Gaulle broadcasts to the nation.

A king of France whose subjects did not yet know him.

EMMANUEL D'ASTIER DE LA VIGERIE:
. . . whose subjects did not exist.

Whose subjects did not exist. . .

ENGLISH NEWSREEL, *outside church:*
*Free French men and women attend a London*
*church service to hear a Requiem sung in honor of*
*the victims of Nazi barbarity in Nantes, and for*
*other martyrs of France. General de Gaulle and*
*Mr. Eden are present at the service.*

ANTHONY EDEN, former Prime Minister of Great
Britain:

There are two things still not fully understood today concerning the status of de Gaulle and the Free French. At that time in London there were several foreign governments—several of them. But de Gaulle was not a government; Free France was not a government. The other nations there in London had come with their governments: the Dutch, the Belgians, the Norwegians, all of them—the governments which had taken refuge with us were the same governments which had once run those countries. But, as you point out yourself, Pétain was still in France, it was a different situation. . . .

Isn't that precisely the most damning condemnation possible of Pétain, of the armistice, of the whole Vichy regime, to see just that? France was the only country to do this, after all. . .

ANTHONY EDEN :
Yes. . . that's true.


PIERRE MENDES-FRANCE, former Prime Minister of France :
Underneath it all, it's true that de Gaulle—precisely because he had no resources, because his army was insignificant, because the French territories that rallied around him were not important—had no other way, there was no other conceivable possibility than for him to be absolutely inflexible in defending those rights of which he was caretaker. . . . Of course, his pride, his harshness, and his often intractable nature didn't make things any easier. I think that, politically speaking, he was right. I don't want any misunderstanding about that. Politically, he was right.


ENGLISH NEWSREEL :
*See this eighteen-year-old French girl coming down a London street. She has just made a dramatic escape from occupied France. After eluding the Gestapo, this brave young patriot sailed 250 miles in an open boat.*

*"Now Mademoiselle X, the microphone is yours."*

*"Oh yes, after my adventure in occupied France I am very happy to be in England. I have already seen General de Gaulle and he promised to give me work to do for the Free French forces in this country. I am very happy in this prospect."*

128.

Pierre Mendès-France, air force lieutenant in '39, had been
accused of desertion by the Vichy government. After the
military tribunal at Clermont-Ferrand convicted him, the
former prime minister escaped from jail and finally reached
London by way of Switzerland.

PIERRE MENDES-FRANCE:
I admit that what happened to me in France gave
me quite a shock. I could not take lightly the insult
of being accused of desertion in the face of the
enemy. I felt the need to fight, the need to prove
myself a fighter. By the time I got to London there
was no question any longer. . . there was no
question. . .

All because they accused you of desertion?

PIERRE MENDES-FRANCE:
Yes, that evening for the first time I found myself
face to face with de Gaulle, who asked me a lot of
questions on what was happening in France. He was
of course very eager for information, he was anxious
to know what French people were thinking, what
their frame of mind was, what sort of will to resist
there was, etc. To find myself in the presence of de
Gaulle, well, I admit it was an overwhelming
experience, it was deeply moving. . . I must say he
received me very well.

It seems that when he received people coming from France
he was often very cold. . .

PIERRE MENDES-FRANCE:
Yes that's true. He is a shy man. His timidity causes
this seemingly cold behavior when he meets people.
Personally I can't complain, maybe because our
conversation was longer. . . .

How was the morale of the Free French?

PIERRE MENDES-FRANCE:
Well, it was a very special army. Few in number
unfortunately, but that was due to circumstance.
First of all, they had all arrived feeling rather
humiliated, it must be admitted. The apparently
legitimate French government, the Vichy
government, had signed the armistice and had

abandoned England altogether. They did not know quite how they would be received when they arrived in England. But it is a fact that they were well received and quickly understood so that most of them felt grateful right away since the English did not make them feel unwelcome. Also, there was great admiration for the English people who had to face the hurricane alone.

The recurring question for French air pilots was the question of whether or not they had the right to bomb France itself. The Lorraine Squadron planes were not long range aircraft, so bombing Berlin was out of the question, and we regretted it. But we were often called on to bomb targets in Belgium, Holland, and France, and that, of course, posed a very cruel dilemma.

A group of Bristol-Bleinheim airplanes above a RAF field.

ENGLISH NEWSREEL:
*The attack on an important power station near Paris
recently carried out by fifty French airmen was
devastating indeed. The choice of fifty Frenchmen to
carry out the attack underlines, of course, the full
recognition of the necessity of bombing targets in
France. The film of this attack which was taken by
the RAF is probably the most vivid of any aerial
pictures taken so far. Watch this film and you will
fly with them. Still at naught feet over the beautiful
countryside of France, the Lorraine Squadron flies
on to do its job.*

PIERRE MENDES-FRANCE :
It was this fear, this persistent question of bombing
France itself, which led us to specialize more and
more in precision bombing—that is, flying at a very
low altitude. It was more risky, but it also permitted
much greater precision. . . .

Doriot gives the salute to PPF guards.

November, 1942: Members of the Parti Populaire Francais
(PPF)—the French fascist party led by Jacques Doriot—
parade down the Champs Elysées.

FRENCH NEWSREEL, *Jacques Doriot, head of the fascist
PPF party, addresses crowd:*
*"England victorious? Half of her merchant
fleet and a third of her navy are lost. England has
already lost Europe, she is losing her small
influence with the Soviet Union, and tomorrow she
will lose her influence in India. England is defeated.
Her only way out is unconditional surrender, but as
a Frenchman I don't enjoy this prospect because
I'm afraid she'll try to clamber onto my back . . ."*

COMTE RENE DE CHAMBRUN, son-in-law of Pierre
Laval:
My father-in-law's real philosophy, which he often
spoke about in private, was that, being a realist, he
had to gain time for our side, at least while Germany
was engaged in conflict with Russia. He thought this
conflict would last a very long time and would allow
France to maintain her place in the world, and to
maintain her empire.

Comte René de Chambrun.

FRENCH NEWSREEL, *Laval at his home in Châteldon:
On April 21st, 1942, in his appeal to France, the head
of the government confided to his listeners: "These
words which I now speak, I have pondered over
here in my native village, in this land of Auvergne
where I was born and to which I remain so
attached ..." But the moments spared his family are
short, and these eight strokes of the clock mark the
beginning of long and laborious hours ahead. Yet he
will still devote a few moments to the villagers who
come here every morning to chat with him.*

**VISIT TO NEARBY FACTORY**

COMTE RENE DE CHAMBRUM:
I am convinced that today the vast majority of the
French people know that Pierre Laval did everything
he could to defend them. I believe this. That is
enough. You walked through this village today and
you questioned people who saw Laval at work, and

not one of them would have made an extremist
accusation against him.

So you knew my father-in-law?

A WORKER :
Yes, I knew him. I knew him well in the period
between 1936 and 1944. The last day I saw him was
the day before he left for Paris. . . . forever. I never
saw him after that. But I used to see him very often,
really, every day when he was at Vichy. We used to
discuss our different problems, mineral waters as
well as problems of the saw mill.

COMTE RENE DE CHAMBRUN :
Did you discuss politics?

A WORKER :
No, never. We never discussed politics. Never.

COMTE RENE DE CHAMBRUN :
Why did the whole of France condemn him at that
time?

A WOMAN :
Not the whole of France, certainly not. I used to go
to the chateau sometimes, to ask for help with my
prisoners of war.

COMTE RENE DE CHAMBRUN, to another worker :
Could you come here? These gentlemen are here in
Châteldon to make a film about the Occupation. How
old were you when the war broke out?

WORKER :
Twenty-five.

COMTE RENE DE CHAMBRUN :
Which regiment were you in?

WORKER :
Twenty-eighth artillery.

COMTE RENE DE CHAMBRUN :
And what happened?

WORKER :
Well, in June, on the 20th of June, we were taken
prisoner. Well, after. . . some hard times, I had the

134.

privilege, thanks to a favor from Monsieur le Premier
Laval, who managed to have me repatriated. . . I
was prisoner. . . I am thankful to him, and to
Madame la Comtesse also.

COMTE RENE DE CHAMBRUN :
When did you come back?

WORKER :
I came back on the 17th of October, 1941. It was a
great favor, because the others stayed until '45 and
even longer. . . .

COMTE RENE DE CHAMBRUN :
You were lucky to be a prisoner from Châteldon,
weren't you?

WORKER :
We were privileged, sir!

1940: Laval at work.

FRENCH NEWSREEL, *Laval commutes to Vichy:*
*Today Monsieur René Bousquet from the Ministry of*
*the Interior has arrived to accompany the head of*
*government on the drive from Châteldon to Vichy,*
*so that the twenty-minute ride can be exploited to*
*full advantage. The Minister of the Interior will*
*present his report in order that President Laval be*
*fully briefed for the decisions he must make later on*
*in the day.*

JACQUES DUCLOS, Communist Party Chief during
occupation:
I say that if the Germans had had to depend only
on the Gestapo, that they could not have done half
the harm they did. Sure, they would have killed
people in the streets, by chance, just anybody—but it
was the French police who helped them... If there
hadn't been any French police to look for
Communists and other patriots—I'm not speaking
just of Communists—well in that case the Germans
would have struck at random, but they would not
have been able to strike such sure, hard blows as they
did against the French Resistance. That is the
truth. ...

FRENCH NEWSREEL, *Laval and Pétain in conference:*
[Laval:] *"Bring me the latest police report you have*
*on hand. ..."*

*Now it is time for the daily conference between the*
*heads of state and government ... All the problems*
*of life in France are discussed candidly by the two*
*men.*

GEORGES LAMIRAND, Secretary of Youth under Pétain:
The Marshal hadn't a jot in common with the
President. The Marshal was a methodical man, while
Laval liked to improvise. The two men had strictly
opposite characters, they were very different men. ...

**What made Marshal Pétain take on Laval in the first**
**place, and then after he was out, to take him on again for**
**a second time?**

GEORGES LAMIRAND:
Well, I think the first time there wasn't much choice,
and that, in fact, it was Laval who made the Marshal
head of state. As for the second time, he was caught
in a tragic situation where the occupying forces
forced Laval upon him.

COMTE RENE DE CHAMBRUN, son-in-law of Pierre Laval:

The Marshal was surrounded by a group of right-wing and extreme right-wing sympathizers, while my father-in-law, let me stress, was a man who you would call today a "man of the center."

GEORGES LAMIRAND:

It's quite obvious that the reason Laval followed a pro-German policy was that he believed in it. Remember that terrible radio broadcast, when Laval said: "I hope for a German victory"? I was in Paris. The next day I was going to meet my family in Auvergne, so I stopped off in Vichy on the way, because I could not comprehend how the head of the French government could say such an awful thing. I saw Laval the next morning and told him: "Mr. President, I am utterly crushed by what you said yesterday on the radio"—"And what did I say?"—You said "I hope for a German victory". "Yes, and then?"—"What do you mean and then?"!!"Well, what did I say afterwards?" "I must admit Mr. President that I was so startled that I don't remember." "I said 'against Bolshevism'."

EMILE COULAUDON, called GASPAR, former leader of the Auvergne maquis:

I was reading an old newspaper recently, *Le Moniteur*, and right across the entire front page ran this headline: "Laval Says"—and he must have chosen the headline himself—since it was his own newspaper after all—"I Hope for a German Victory." Well, there were a lot of interpretations of what he meant by this hope for a German victory; some people said: "Yes, but don't forget that Laval added 'because I am fighting against Communism.'" Now in France, while it's true that we may not all be Communists—and that's why we fought after all, so that every one would have the right to his own ideas—well, we certainly cannot be anti-Communists, because being anti-Communist is already being anti-something, so that then one could go on saying: well, the Freemasons—I am not a Freemason, by the way—the Freemasons should be put in concentration camps. Or the Jews: you were born Jewish so you should be sent to the gas chambers. . . .

**During your relatively long stay in Clermont-Ferrand, did you ever see or hear anyone mention any persecutions?**

HELMUT TAUSEND, Captain of the Wehrmacht in Clermont:
No, I saw nothing and heard nothing.

**How is that possible? You don't deny that persecution of Jews—die Juden in German—took place?**

HELMUT TAUSEND:
You mean *jugend*, "young people," or *Juden*, "the Jews"?

**Die Juden. Jews.**

HELMUT TAUSEND:
Well, as far as Jews were concerned, we really could not know to what extent they had been able to infiltrate the partisan resistance groups. In any case it wasn't up to us, the army, to deal with the Jews.

September, 1941: Jews bring in their radios to police precinct station for registration.

COMTE RENE DE CHAMBRUN, son-in-law of Pierre Laval:
In all countries occupied by Germany, except for France, the number of Jews arrested and deported —the number of Jews who never came back—is terrifying. In 1946 only 5.8 percent had survived. But if you take the statistics for French Jews alone, a statistic which no one disputes, it shows that only 5 percent *did not* come back. In the army for instance...

I'm sorry to interrupt. I'm quite familiar with that statistic, and it refers only to those French Jews who had not lost their citizenship. It so happens that, of those Jews without citizenship—that is, foreign Jews, or Jews whose citizenship had been stripped away by the Vichy government—that indeed only 5 percent came back: in effect, the same percentage as in other countries. So let me ask you this question: does a statesman, even one who is trying to salvage for better or worse as well as he can, does any statesman have the right to choose in this way between two groups of human beings?

COMTE RENE DE CHAMBRUN, son-in-law of Pierre Laval:
The situation is a tragic and dramatic one where one has to save the greatest number of human lives possible.

CLAUDE LEVY, author and biologist:
I come from a middle class background, I went to the Lycée Pasteur but the question of being Jewish ... we were not religious people. When I was told by others that I was a Jew, I was, at first, extremely saddened to feel rejected from my national community and from the country I loved, not because I was brought up in it, but because I had learned to love it by reading its history which I found beautiful. Then I became interested in the Jews.

I think that quibbling over figures is, in effect, a way of trying to balance the accounts in an area where this kind of thing cannot be allowed. The fact that a French government agreed to surrender French nationals and even refugees who sought its protection—thus denying the traditional right to asylum in France—proves that it was not a government worthy of being labelled French, or worthy of what is loved about this country, about France. France collaborated. It is the *only* country in Europe which collaborated. Others signed armistices, capitulated in the field and so on, but France is the only country in Europe which had a government which collaborated, a government which introduced laws on the racist level that went even further than the Nürenberg Laws—French racial criteria were even more demanding than German racial criteria—so it's not a very pretty chapter of French history. Perhaps it is to be expected therefore that school books would present only the more glorious side of the story. But historically it is certainly false.

I was arrested because I was in the Resistance—in the FTP, the "Francs Tireurs et Partisans." I was arrested during a hold-up.

**You were sixteen years old?**

CLAUDE LEVY :
Seventeen. I was arrested by the French police. They

Claude Levy.

didn't torture me, though they did question me for eighteen days running in a, let's say, physical manner. I remained in French prison for a year. In the courtyard of that prison I saw seventeen of my comrades shot by firing squads of French gendarmes, and on July the 2nd, 1944, I was handed over to the S.S. with all my fellow prisoners by the French Department of Prisons—the only prison administration in Europe to ever make the despicable gesture of handing over prison inmates, bound hand and foot, to the Germans. I was deported on a train called the "death train," so called because it was en route for two months, until finally it was attacked and machine gunned by British planes who did not know that it contained deportees.

I was able to escape on the 25th of August 1944, and the train arrived in Dachau on the 27th. That's when I heard that my parents had been. . . . I looked for them and heard that they had been deported. France was covered with concentration camps: Lurs, Argèles, Rivesaltes, Drancy, at any rate, there were a lot of them. There were not only Jews; there were also Spanish Republicans, Freemasons, gypsies, and all of these people were handed over to the Germans in small bundles as the Germans requested them and as trains became available.

The people who took part in this persecution were quite numerous, not to mention those who participated indirectly for some minor personal gain and were happy to see a competitor disappear: we found for instance 137 denunciations by French people left in the files of the Office for Jewish Affairs, and let me tell you that half of them were doctors denouncing Monsieur so-and-so to the Gestapo or to the Office for Jewish Affairs because they didn't like the competition.

One fine summer day the Parisian police, supervised by the S.S. and Gestapo units in occupied territories, organized a day of arrests of the Jews in Paris. This was to enter the sad history of racial persecution under the name of ''the Vél d'Hiv Round Up.''

CLAUDE LEVY:
At this time the Germans did not plan to arrest anybody under sixteen—no children. But the Parisian police who carried out the raid of July 16th, 1942, with a zeal beyond the call of duty—they were

praised by the Germans at any rate—went ahead and arrested children anyway. And so there were 4,051 children at the Vélodrome d'Hiver, crying and dirtying their pants, posing serious problems to the social workers, who were mostly Quakers or Protestant women.

Since it hadn't been planned to deport these children at all—the Germans hadn't planned to anyway—and since the parents had already been deported to camps at Pithiviers and Beaune-la-Rolande, thus separating the children from their parents while a decision was patiently awaited, Eichmann, or rather Röthke, who was Eichmann's representative in France, sent a telegram to Berlin to ask what should be done with these children. And while they were waiting, Laval is reputed to have said: "The children will have to be deported too". This is reported in a telegram by Danneker, who was a security officer in France, and anyone can see it—it's in the archives. The telegram is authenticated, in my opinion, by two factors: one, by the conversation between Pastor Beugner and Laval. Pastor Beugner, who had gone to see Laval to plead for the children, reports: "When I spoke of the children, in particular of the possibility of having them evacuated, perhaps to America, Laval replied: 'It does not matter, it is of no importance, I am carrying out the prophylaxis.' "

Monsieur Xavier Vallat, Commissioner for Jewish Questions.

Two young women wearing the Jewish star.

MARCEL VERDIER, pharmacist in Clermont:
I'm sorry to interrupt when not asked, but if these
children had only seen, as I did, these poor people—
men, women, children, old and young, piled into
trucks, pushed about, piled like human cattle—and
I knew where they were going, I knew... there was
only one thing to do, and these young people they
would have done as I did if they'd seen it; they
would have taken their handkerchiefs and told
their employees: "I'm sorry, I've got to go out for
a couple of minutes," and they would have gone to
the basement to cry.

**Does anti-Semitism still exist in Auvergne?**

A YOUNG GIRL:
Yes, just as much as then.

**In what ways can you tell? What makes you say that—do
you hear people talking that way?**

YOUNG GIRL:
I don't know. For example one might say of someone:
"Oh he's a Yid, he's a Jew".

This happens among the students of Clermont?

YOUNG GIRL :
Oh yes.

Do you think that may be because people don't talk
enough about the German occupation?

MARCEL VERDIER :
In a large family like mine—we have seven children
—the father is preoccupied with only one thing :
making money. There's no time for any family
conversation, there's no family life, because
everything goes too quickly in modern society because
we need money.

What about these children? Did any of them come back?
What percentage?

CLAUDE LEVY, author and biologist :
It is believed that none of the children ever came
back. I made inquiries—and so did others—on what
happened when the children arrived at the camp :
They were shot at once.

COMTE RENE DE CHAMBRUN, son-in-law of Pierre
Laval :
My father-in-law was anti-repression. It is a well
known fact today.

FRENCH NEWSREEL, *Laval at work in Vichy:*
*When the last of audiences has ended, the day is still*
*not over for Pierre Laval. The Hotel Matignon is*
*now quiet and the President, alone, knows he will*
*start again tomorrow his work on the objective he*
*has defined for himself.*

*"I see before me only the necessary task*
*ahead, and I will not give it up until the safety of*
*France is assured. I ask you to understand the*
*meaning of this task and to sustain my effort."*

**VISIT TO THE CASTLE OF SIGMARINGEN, MAY, 1969.**

TOUR GUIDE :
In 1944 Hitler gave the owner and his family

twenty-four hours notice to vacate the castle. He ordered the Vichy government installed here immediately. Pétain and Laval stayed until the capitulation.

CHRISTIAN DE LA MAZIERE, former volunteer in the French Waffen S.S.:
I came here with two other volunteers, friends of mine. We were just back from Yanovitz, near Prague, where we had been taking an anti-tanks training course, and we wanted to ask Marshal Pétain, who we knew was there, a very particular question. The question was. . . whether or not the point we had by then come to was a logical one and if it were indeed necessary to take the plunge and. . . leave for the Eastern Front.

**Exactly what point had you come to by then?**

CHRISTIAN DE LA MAZIERE:
Well, to the point of wearing German uniforms which, after all, neither our education, nor even really the desire for change we had held while young had prepared us for.

We arrived here, we presented ourselves at the castle, and we asked to see the Marshal. He had French guards, French gendarmes. Our request was passed along to the Marshal, but it was useless. He refused to see us.

**And Laval?**

CHRISTIAN DE LA MAZIERE:
We were not allowed to see President Laval either.

**How did that affect you deep down? It was a sort of repudiation after all, quite a serious repudiation, since you had the right to imagine some connection at least between those people who were defending a certain set of policies, and you, who were in some way or another, applying them.**

CHRISTIAN DE LA MAZIERE:
Yes, it was a total, a brutal repudiation. In fact, it almost provoked us into leaving at once and joining our comrades in Wilflecken to go to the Eastern Front, and *just have done with it*. We no longer had any illusions. It's difficult to speak for 7,000 other young men—and let's make it quite clear, there were 7,000 young men, from all walks of life,

145.

who fought on the Eastern Front in the Charlemagne Division. . . . It is said that there were only 300 survivors, and I believe it. You simply can't deny it, say it isn't important. The majority of these 7,000 were not at all, as I said before, prepared to wear this uniform, particularly not the most extreme uniform. . . .

Christian de la Maziére in 1969 at Sigmaringen Castle. At his left is interviewer André Harris.

**You mean the uniform of the Waffen S.S.?**

CHRISTIAN DE LA MAZIERE:
Yes, the uniform of the Waffen S.S.

**And the French of Vichy greeted you in this uniform as if you were the symbol of. . .**

CHRISTIAN DE LA MAZIERE:
. . . of something rather embarrassing, something which was going to demand some explanation at a

later date. And you know that, in the years that followed, some of the Vichy people tried to explain it away as nothing but part of a political strategy that, in the final analysis, really wasn't that serious. Well, it surprised me... you know... when 7,000 young men, some of whom could some day have become the nation's leaders, let themselves be slaughtered in uniform, well, I personally think that that is a rather serious matter.

In order to understand various people's sense of commitment during the war, one must go back at least to 1934. By that time there wasn't a single high school or lycée in France which wasn't constantly undergoing riots and disruption. By '34, there had been some extremely violent political battles in the heart of the lycée. In the editorials of *Gringoire,* of *Candide,* or *l'Action Française, Le Populaire, l'Humanité,* people were constantly being encouraged to slaughter one another. The military people pictured themselves as the guardians of a certain tradition... they were very right-wing.

**In February '34, the crucial year of political battles in pre-war France, how old were you?**

CHRISTIAN DE LA MAZIERE :
I was going on thirteen years old.

**You were only thirteen and already that politically minded?**

CHRISTIAN DE LA MAZIERE :
Yes, people kept preaching revolution; and for people of our social class there was really no choice, we couldn't choose the Communist Party, so we had to choose the other party of revolution. And what was that? Fascism. We keep hearing a lot about anti-Semitism.... You shouldn't forget that my whole youth was drenched in an atmosphere of violent anti-Semitism. And then we were also influenced by the fact of all the deaths in February, '34. It was the beginning of revolution; France was split down the middle—don't forget about that.

**Has the fear of Communism played a great part in your... ?**

CHRISTIAN DE LA MAZIERE :
Yes.

. . . political awareness, your political consciousness?

CHRISTIAN DE LA MAZIERE:
Something happened beyond our borders then which
was a terribly important. Just as certain people's
political consciousness has been shaped by the war
in Algeria, so was ours shaped by the Spanish
Civil War. How could a boy of my age, brought up
in my kind of family, have failed to become strongly
anti-Communist, especially when newspapers, when
the newspapers I read, were full of pictures of nuns
being shot, Carmelite nuns being disinterred, tombs
being defaced, etc. It was. . .

The backdrop to your political consciousness.

CHRISTIAN DE LA MAZIERE:
Yes, indeed it was.

And as far as Fascism was concerned, how did it strike
you intellectually? Did you realize what it meant?

Paris, in front of the Arc de Triomphe: ceremony of the
Franquiste Congress, a pro-Franco fascist group.

148.

CHRISTIAN DE LA MAZIERE:
Only vaguely, I must admit, vaguely. But for us it
was also a form of rebellion against our families.
The first impression we got from Nüremberg seemed
to us a sort of birth, the birth of a new religion. I
use the word ''mass'' now regularly because it really
was like a mass. In every political ideology, there is
a religious core. . . if people, especially young people,
are not taken with a certain decorum, a certain
style. . .

[Tour of the Castle continues] :

TOUR GUIDE:
Here is the motto of the Hohenzollern family: *Nihil
sine Deo*: Nothing without God. Dining room, then
corridor. . .

CHRISTIAN DE LA MAZIERE:
I was contacted by members of the Resistance at
that time. It was when they were looking for recruits.
It's true, I have no excuse, really, I was asked
several times to join the Resistance, to join the true
Resistance. My idea at the time, the idea of a young
man, was that there were only two ideologies which
could change the world: one which had already done
it—Marxism; and the other, which was the ideology
of National-Socialism.

**Would it bother you if one were to say that, in 1941, you
were a young Facist?**

CHRISTIAN DE LA MAZIERE :
No, it wouldn't bother me.

**Very well then.**

**You were on the side which ran no risk of persecution. Were
you particularly proud of being on that side, considering
what France was like at the time?**

CHRISTIAN DE LA MAZIERE :
You are right to ask that question concerning
persecutions. It is something which is very important
to me. I don't want to pretend I didn't know. I
did know, I knew that Jews were being arrested.
Though I assure you that I never thought, I never
imagined extermination. . . .

**That it all ended in Auschwitz?**

CHRISTIAN DE LA MAZIERE:
Never.

**So you thought that it was simply a matter of putting them out of public life?**

CHRISTIAN DE LA MAZIERE:
Well, I presumed they were put in camps of course.
But there were many people in camps at the time.
After all, there were two million French prisoners in
Germany. You see, I thought prisoner-of-war camps
and camps for political prisoners were about the same
thing.

FRENCH NEWSREEL, *Jacques Doriot addresses a large
audience:*
*"Let's put the cards on the table: if France
is to remain a European power and a world power,
if France wants to remain worthy of Europe, then
she must join in the fight against Bolshevism. There
is no way out!"*

FRENCH NEWSREEL, *people standing before
storefronts:*
*Recruiting offices for the League against Bolshevism
opened up both in the occupied and non-occupied
zone. Bolshevism defeated will mean a united
Europe!*

CHRISTIAN DE LA MAZIERE:
Remember there were recruiting offices all over
France. Executive orders had been signed, and they
can't be denied either. I know we're like the plague
to them today. There exists today a certain political
strategy carried on by former Vichy supporters—
who have, since the Liberation, joined back up with
the various majorities. This group explains very
matter-of-factly that both extreme Gaullism and
extreme Communism were the danger at the time,
and that we were another danger—we, the
bloodthirsty toughs, the "super" collaborationists . . .

**What was your first contact with the reality of the German
military, not the myth?**

CHRISTIAN DE LA MAZIERE:
Reality came right there in the training schools for
the Waffen S.S. It was rather special, quite a new
experience, really, there was a mythology. . . . It

made us grin, but at the same time we admired it. . . you know we Latins were confronted with all this German mythology, these "oaths between two chains," these postulates like "my honor is named Fidelity," and other things which both fascinated us and made us smirk a bit. But the Frenchman stays a Frenchman, even in his convictions. Anyway, the Germans realized this, and they didn't take us very seriously.

March 1943: At Versailles, the "Legion of French Volunteers" holds a ceremony in memory of its members departed for the Front.

**And what were your relations with the Germans like? What did you call them?**

CHRISTIAN DE LA MAZIERE:
*"Les Chleus"*—the Krauts—I don't think I knew a single Frenchman in the Charlemagne Division who called them anything else.

**Well, then it was off to a bad start, wasn't it??**

CHRISTIAN DE LA MAZIERE:
And most of us called Hitler "le grand Jules." But that's the Frenchman after all, like that—"le grand Jules."

**Was there much of a spirit of a real united European army among the foreign Waffen S.S. units?**

CHRISTIAN DE LA MAZIERE:
Well you know, we took part mostly—if I dare say so—in the defeat. In greatness you can develop a certain spirit, but in defeat. . . . All I know is that the Germans reserved for us some of the best available seats at exactly the moment the Eastern Front collapsed, when Rokossovsky and Zhoukov had cut the German front into several chunks, several pieces. And that's when German headquarters decided to stuff its pockets with the foreign units of the Waffen S.S. . . .

I have the suspicion they wanted to get rid of something that might be cumbersome in future negotiations. . .

**And contacts with the German people? Were there any?**

CHRISTIAN DE LA MAZIERE:
Oh yes, that's the one great memory I have left. Before meeting up with the Russians, we first ran into a group of refugees. It was worse than '40. All of Eastern Prussia and a part of Pomerania were fleeing to the center of Germany.

**And what did they tell you?**

CHRISTIAN DE LA MAZIERE:
Well, they offered us their daughters, saying they preferred to have them with us than with the Russians. . . . We saw the Germans retreating, we were there to protect their retreat. . . . It was a new turn in history, and it was sort of funny. It almost made us laugh—it amused us for a while, but only briefly, because the Russians soon brought us back to a more healthy view of the state of things. . .

**Were medals still being handed out to you at that time? Did you take part, or at least benefit, from this distribution?**

CHRISTIAN DE LA MAZIERE:
Yes.

**What was given out, the Iron Cross?**

CHRISTIAN DE LA MAZIERE:
The Iron Cross, First and Second Class.

**Has everything you learned from the last war, especially about National-Socialism, which as you said held a certain fascination for you at the time, has all this led you to revise your judgment of the alternatives in those days?**

CHRISTIAN DE LA MAZIERE:
Yes, of course. Only fools never modify or change their opinions. I take the responsibility for myself only, of course. I have changed, but that's another story. . . Young people ask me what I think about commitment, about their own sense of commitment today. It's always attractive, commitment, fascinating because it is a change, but sometimes it also has dramatic consequences. So I must admit. . . I advise caution. . .

**Have you become a liberal? Are you somewhat afraid of ideologies?**

CHRISTIAN DE LA MAZIERE:
A little. . . Even a lot.

June 6, 1944, D-Day: the Allied landing at Normandy.

Above: American GI's in place de la Concorde. At top right: After the liberation of Paris, white flags hang from houses occupied by Germans on rue Castiglione. Bottom right: German officers surrendering in front of the Opéra in Paris.

154

155.

Paris, Liberation Day: while Parisians prepare to celebrate the arrival of the Allies, a sniper spreads panic on place de la Concorde.

November 11, 1944: Churchill and de Gaulle on the Champs Elysées.

[Georges Brassens sings, "The beautiful girl who slept with the King of Prussia had her scalp shaved clean."]

MARCEL VERDIER, pharmacist in Clermont:
Personally, my own flesh and blood never suffered from the occupation; they never killed my wife, they never killed my children. My friend Menut's feelings are totally different from mine of course: they took his wife and they tortured her, they tore off her nipples—and that's no joke—they burned her with a red hot iron... they committed all sorts of atrocities on her. So Menut's feelings are naturally totally different from my own. . . .

Paris, 1944: French police constables massacred by the Germans prior to the Liberation.

COMMANDANT MENUT, Resistance leader in Clermont:
The spinal column was entirely exposed by
horsewhipping—entirely.

**How do you know all this?**

COMMANDANT MENUT:
From two women: Madame Michelin who was
sharing the cell with her—I think it was Madame
Michelin anyway—and Madame Martineau, from
Volvic. Actually, it was also one of them who enabled
me to identify her body, when she told me: ''There
are her slippers, I am sure it must be her, I made
those slippers for her just before they took her away
to shoot her.''

**At that point you weren't able to identify her?**

COMMANDANT MENUT:
No. First of all they didn't shoot her at all—they
buried her without. . .

**Without a coffin?**

COMMANDANT MENUT:
Without a coffin, yes, but. . . they buried her without
killing her off first, she was still in a coma from the
beatings, and nobody even thought of finishing her
off. She was kicked around, beaten. . . I think I'm
entitled to say this because one of the torturers
himself told me that he had pushed a broom handle
into her vagina.

MATHEUS BLEIBINGER, Wehrmacht soldier stationed in
Auvergne:
Some were very vengeful against us, and some were
not. It depended mostly on whether a father or a
son had been killed or taken prisoner. The ones whose
relatives were prisoners in Germany thought they
were being ill-treated, even though that wasn't
the case. Well, they were angry. Anyway, that's
the way it was.

I was taken prisoner by the maquis. In October
of '44 they took me to Clermont-Ferrand where I
was to be put in a camp next to the train station. At
ten in the morning I was taken off the train and
strapped to a stretcher, since I had been wounded.

I stayed there all day on the platform of the train station. That's where the station was, and over there was the main building, there the prisoners' camp. In the evening nurses came to take me away with a cart. All day long meanwhile, civilians had come by to get a look at me, lying there on the stretcher; some spat on me, and some took pity on me, it seemed.

**What were you thinking, what did you feel, while you were laying there on the platform of the Clermont train station?**

MATHEUS BLEIBINGER:
Well, I thought it wasn't very nice, that it was an awful thing for them to do, they should have realized that the same thing could have happened to their father or their son. And what would they have said then?

Members of the **FFI** liberate the region around Chartres.

**You were bound by ropes to the stretcher?**

MATHEUS BLEIBINGER:
Yes, I couldn't move. That frustrated me because I
knew Clermont-Ferrand like the inside of my pocket,
and I would have been able to hide. . . I had a girl
friend in Saint-Césaire.

**And that's where you would have gone?**

MATHEUS BLEIBINGER:
Probably, yes. In any event she was a very sweet
young girl who was not anti-German, and very
proper, mind you.

---

MADAME SOLANGE, hairdresser outside Clermont:
It was in August '44, I was spending the summer
holiday at my mother's. I was spending the holidays
with my mother, in August, when a carload of
civilians came to take me away. There were flags
everywhere, but of course they had machine guns
too. I hadn't realized quite how things were going
in this little village of Chateaugué, since it was all
very quiet. But when we arrived in Clermont I
realized how different things were—they were
arresting people everywhere, and it wasn't a pretty
sight. So I was locked up in the cellars of La Poterne,
a fortress in Clermont-Ferrand. There were women
there in their nightgowns, and others still wearing
their underwear—they'd been pulled out of bed and
arrested in the middle of the night. I myself didn't
know why I had been arrested. Not at all. We were
to be taken before a tribunal of some sort. When
some of the women came back their heads were
shaven. They were the ones who went with the
Germans. I. . . Well *I* certainly had never done that!

**You never went out with the Germans?**

MADAME SOLANGE:
No, never!

**So, what were you accused of then?**

MADAME SOLANGE:
Well, I was arrested. . . . I found out a month later.
I stayed one whole month in jail, in the prison at

Clermont-Ferrand, without knowing why I was there. Many times I asked the commissioned officers—they were temporary officers, of course—why I was there, what they could tell me about my situation. And they all said, after they had first asked my name: "Well no, we have no record of anything against that name, maybe it's a mistake, just be patient, it's a mess here now, and you'll certainly be freed very soon" . . . . There were a lot of French Resistance soldiers, FFI, there and I was told I had been arrested because of a letter of denunciation.

Someone had denounced a captain, a friend, he was a friend of mine, his wife was also a friend of mine; in fact, it was his wife who was really my friend; they were people my own age, from my part of the country. There had been a denunciation, which had been intercepted by the Gestapo of Chamalière, and it was that denunciation which had led to my arrest.

Paris 1945: woman who collaborated with Germans is paraded naked through the streets after the Liberation.

Women collaborators being led through the crowds, heads shaven and chests painted with swastikas.

**And in fact you were not really guilty?**

MADAME SOLANGE:
Not at all! And I kept denying it of course. They came a second time and this time they took me from the prison to a building in the place de Lille. A man stripped me, and there was a tub there, full of water—he plunged me into the tub. I held on with my hands, but they handcuffed my hands behind my back. I held on with my head, but they punched me on the chin, and I sank to the bottom. I had to swallow water then, because when you are under water you have to swallow water. They realized I was weakening, so the man grabbed me by the hair, pulled my head out of the water, and put his finger in my mouth. I threw up all the water I had swallowed, and he asked: ''Well, do you confess or

Woman collaborator on the streets of Chartres.

don't you?'' Well no, I couldn't confess to something
I hadn't done. At that moment I regretted not
having done anything, let me assure you... it was
such an awful thing.

**But who were all these people? You keep saying
''someone,'' ''some individuals.'' Do you think that perhaps
some of the police had done this sort of thing before, under
a different government?**

MADAME SOLANGE:
Oh, I don't know; and then...

**But, you come from Clermont, you must know some of these
people...**

MADAME SOLANGE:
That's just it. I never saw any of these people again
... I think they must have been people who came in
especially to rough up other people. I don't know.

**During the occupation, you were... you were for Marshal
Pétain?**

MADAME SOLANGE:
Yes, I was for the Marshal.

**Why?**

MADAME SOLANGE:
I was for the Marshal, I don't know, I wasn't
political. . . I was for the Marshal.

**So, why did all this happen?**

MADAME SOLANGE:
This friend, this man, had been denounced to the
Gestapo, and the letter was intercepted by the post
office of Chamalière.

**Do you have any idea who could have copied your
handwriting?**

MADAME SOLANGE:
The wife.

**The wife. She was the one who denounced you?**

MADAME SOLANGE:
She was the one! I asked the captain about it then.
I asked the captain. . . I don't remember anymore. . .
I went on trial. Captain Mury was the first witness.
The judge asked him: "It seems that your wife
enjoys imitating her friends' handwriting?"—
"Yes, sometimes, but she does not do it well. Besides,
the accused is taking advantage of that to cast
suspicion on my wife." Then when his wife came
up to be a witness, the judge asked her the same
question. She answered: "Never." Then the judge
told her: "But madame, we were just told that you
did, a few minutes ago on the witness stand." She
turned to me, thinking it was me who had said it,
and she said: "Oh sure, she has a good memory!"
The judge thumped on his desk then and said: "But
madame, it was your husband who just said it!"
Then she began stammering, and she said: "Yes,
well sometimes I do, when the handwriting is very
beautiful." A ripple went through the court at that
moment. The people who were for me—I had some
friends of course, although there were also enemies,
those for and those against—my friends all told me
later: "I can assure you that at the moment we were

sure there would at least be a further investigation to find out what sort of a forger she was.'' But there was nothing more. And I got fifteen years.

**When you say you had both friends and enemies in the court room, would you say in general that those friends and enemies could be distinguished along the lines of differing attitudes during the occupation?**

MADAME SOLANGE:
No. . . no. . . no.

**What I mean is—were your enemies people who called themselves ''resisters''?**

MADAME SOLANGE:
Yes, in a way. They were not personal enemies, they simply were not on our side. I was for the Marshal and they were on the other side. That's all, I think.

**When you were in there in that tub full of water, did you ever think that maybe, while you had been more or less supporting the Vichy regime, the same sort of thing was happening to other people?**

MADAME SOLANGE:
Oh I don't know. I didn't try to look so far. . .

**You were frank enough to admit you were for Pétain. Did your Catholic beliefs influence you in that direction?**

MADAME SOLANGE:
No.

**Then what did it stem from? Your support for Pétain?**

MADAME SOLANGE:
Well maybe it was the Marshal's ideas.

**Which ideas?**

MADAME SOLANGE:
What he wanted to do for France. And I thought he was a very fine man.

**Do you still think so?**

MADAME SOLANGE:
Yes, I do.

You thus defended many people accused by the powers that be during the Vichy regime, and then, after the Liberation, you defended those accused by the new powers that be.

MAITRE HENRI ROCHAT , lawyer in Clermont:
Yes, it did seem strange to some people who were poorly informed. But it's obvious that we, as lawyers, always take the side of the accused, and, of course, when political power changes, those accused are no longer the same. It was an extremely brutal period.

In the three or four days following the liberation of Clermont, I think that perhaps 1200 people were arrested, and out of them only 600 reached prison. You can imagine what happened to the other 600. And those who had trials then received a very summary sort of justice, which might as well have

August 1944: Execution of a collaborator. Men collaborators were often shot on the spot.

been dispensed with, considering the atrocious things being punished.

I was involved in the trial of three miliciens, Vichy police, who were accused of—and they had confessed to it—arresting young maquisards, plucking their eyes out, placing live maybugs in their sockets, and sewing up the eyelids. Faced with that sort of thing one wonders if a trial is necessary at all. It might have been better to just shoot them at once. Judgment *was* reached quickly, and quite a few *were* shot. And later on, of course, it turned out there were a lot of judicial errors in the sense that, because of the fervor of the Liberation, people were condemned to death and executed who certainly did not deserve it. On the other hand, after about a month or six weeks, courts of justice were set up, presided over by professional magistrates and complete with juries, like a Court of Sessions. And in these trials, I must say, I don't think there were any judicial errors, if you are first willing to grant that one may condemn to death someone who denounced another countryman who was deported and never returned. At the time such things simply could not be forgiven.

After the Liberation, Emmanuel d'Astier de la Vigerie addresses a crowd.

FRENCH NEWSREEL, *Emmanuel d'Astier de la Vigerie speaks to a large audience:*
*"Let the heads of traitors roll—that is justice!*
*Let the property of all collaborators, of*
*all powerful landlords, banks, and trusts who*
*betrayed their country be seized—that is justice!"*

FRENCH NEWSREEL, *Monsieur Guyot of the Communist party addresses a crowd:*
*"If France is ever to be free, then we cannot permit one German or one traitor to remain on our land!"*

**Mr. Eden, during this interview it seems you tend to be rather charitable towards Marshal Pétain in general. Do you think today that his being condemned after the Liberation was an unfair step?**

ANTHONY EDEN, former Prime Minister of Great Britain:
Ah, well, that is not something that an Englishman can pronounce on, that really is not... no... For this simple reason: that if one hasn't been through— as our people mercifully did not go through—the horror of an occupation by a foreign power, you have no right to pronounce upon what a country does which has been through all that.

EMMANUEL D'ASTIER DE LA VIGERIE, former Secretary of State, resister:
I myself was not shocked when de Gaulle said: "We must still pay our respect to the Marshal of Verdun." I don't give a damn what he said. It seems to me quite natural. It is one aspect of French history and we must accept French history as it comes. But we must not keep partisanship and divisive quarrels alive forever. You don't solve the problem by killing a man, especially five or ten, or two years after he has committed the crime. They shouldn't be left free, or allowed to hold responsible positions or to participate in political activities. But they mustn't be turned into heroes available for future use, that's all.

Of course, that's a very personal opinion. I think few resisters would speak the way I do.

**Where does this present calm, this rejection of partisanship come from? How do you explain the new turn in your evolution?**

EMMANUEL D'ASTIER DE LA VIGERIE:
Well, it's funny, maybe it sounds like nonsense— but really it's because I was afraid. Throughout

168.

the Resistance years I was afraid; blind heroes like
General Massu... are very removed from me, you
know, I would never have thought of committing
suicide, I love life....

SHOT OF TOMBSTONE:
Emmanuel d'Astier de la Vigerie
Born February 6th, 1900
Died June 12th, 1969
Compagnon de la libération pour la guerre '39–'45
Chevalier de la Légion d'Honneur


**AT THE GRAVES' FARMHOUSE NEAR CLERMONT:**

**You were denounced to the Germans?**

LOUIS GRAVE:
Yes I was denounced... I've got a pretty good idea
of who it was, but...

**And you've never been tempted to take revenge?**

LOUIS GRAVE:
What's the use?

**Well after all, it would be a natural enough reaction.**

LOUIS GRAVE:
When I first came back I might almost have been
tempted.... But then I said: "It's not worth it."
I remember that one day at police headquarters in
Clermont someone said to me, "What do you want to
do, want to get even? I know who did it. If you want,
either we or your pals will do it for you, and we'll
never give you the name." And I said, "I know the
name." He asked who had told me. "Nobody. I
found out for myself. And if I wanted to get even,
I would have done it myself by now!"

**But what is it like then to have neighbors in your village
or nearby who are informers—having to live with these
people? Does one forget, or...?**

LOUIS GRAVE:
Oh no, you never forget, it stays engraved in your
memory.... but what can you do? Nothing.


HELMUT TAUSEND:

This is the Iron Cross, and this is the Merit Cross, with the sword—Merit Cross second class—this is a medal for infantry in close-combat zones, this is the Eastern Front medal which we used to call "the frozen meat medal," and this is the Loyal Service badge, for four years of loyal service.

**The Loyal Service badge. . .**

HELMUT TAUSEND:
Yes, for serving four years of war.

**You must know, I am sure, that there are quite a few people in Germany today who refuse to wear those decorations because they were awarded by the Nazi state. But you don't mind wearing them on an occasion like this one?**

**Mr. and Mrs. Helmut Tausend.**

HELMUT TAUSEND:
Yes, you're right, there are some people who would

not approve of this, but. . . but please take a look at
those people, they're usually men who were never
in action, who were never soldiers, who never had
the chance to earn any medals.

**Do you think that that's the only reason—that those who
don't wear medals do so because they don't have them?**

HELMUT TAUSEND :
Yes, because they don't have them. Besides, today
medals are awarded again in this country. So what's
the difference between today's medals and
yesterday's medals?

MATHEUS BLEIBINGER, Wehrmacht soldier stationed in
Auvergne:
As we say in Bavaria, ''There was a worm in the
fruit.'' We aren't fools, but we did lose the war. But
today, we're not sure that it wasn't better that way.
After all if we had won, Hitler might have gone on,
and where would we be today? Maybe having
occupation duty somewhere in Africa or even in
America.

MARCEL VERDIER, pharmacist in Clermont:
I was sent on a mission with that motorbike of mine,
and I was carrying in my pocket a Beretta pistol,
entrusted to me by my friend Bessoux. I don't think
he gave it to me as a gift so much as a way of getting
rid of it because he was scared, you know. So here I
was with this famous Beretta in my pocket, and on
the way to the White Gully, what do I see? A
German column had just passed along ahead of me,
and there was a poor German ''Boche,'' dyspeptic,
doddering, white-haired—he hadn't had a haircut in
ages—his helmet was too small, he was dressed
pitifully, and his motorbike had broken down. He
made signs at me, for me to stop. I looked at him.
I was three meters away from him, with the gun in
my pocket, and I felt like treating myself to one
Boche before it was over. Then I looked at him more
closely, and, well. . . his dolman was buttoned up
and the buttons. . . he was so fat that the buttons
were all popping. . . and after all it would seem
more like killing a pig, which isn't very interesting.
I didn't. I just let him go. He asked me something
about a monkey wrench, which I didn't understand,

Maurice Chevalier visits a French prisoner camp inside Germany.

I don't speak German, so then I saluted him and
left him there. I don't know what became of him.
Well that's what I had to tell you.

**What if you had killed him then, would you regret it now?**

MARCEL VERDIER:
Certainly, and though I didn't kill him in the end,
I did think about it. . . .

........................................................................................................................

NEWSREEL, *Maurice Chevalier addresses his American
fans:*
*"Hello everybody! Here is your old friend
Maurice Chevalier speaking to you from Paris
where I was born.*
*"Ladies and gentlemen, sometime ago, they said
in the newspapers and the radio, that I had been
killed, yes, they said once I had been killed in a
railroad accident, then, they said, that I had been
shot by the Gestapo, then they said that I had been
shot by the patriots, then they said I had been shot
by the militians. Well you see, for a man who has
been shot so many times, I don't feel so bad. Well,
there is something I would like to make clear to you.*

*"At the end of '41 a false propaganda made the
people of France and of the whole world believe that
as an artist I had made a tour of Germany during
the German occupation of France. I want to say that
it is absolutely untrue, I have never made a tour of
Germany whatsoever. I just accepted to go and sing
in a prisoner camp in Germany, a French prisoners'
camp where I had been a prisoner myself in the last
war. I just sang there one afternoon to cheer up the
boys, and I never sang anywhere else. I hope that
France will soon recover and I also hope that very
soon also I'll be able to come up and see you
sometimes if only for a change. Well, waiting for
that, I can't help thinking of a song that I used to
sing sometimes ago when I was in your country
and that song went about like this: I don't play the
piano, so excuse me, I sing without the piano:"*

> *Let the whole world sigh or cry*
> *I'll be high in the sky*
> *Up on top of a rainbow,*
> *Sweeping the clouds away.*

*Don't go on hoping, moping,*
*Happiness will come.*

*That's not the way*
*It does not pay*
*If you want happiness*
*Just help yourself to some*
*Why don't you try to*
*Take life the way I do.*

*Let the whole world sigh or cry*
*I'll be high in the sky*
*Up on top of a rainbow,*
*Sweeping the clouds away.*

*I don't care what's down below*
*Let it rain*
*Let it snow*
*I'll be up on a rainbow,*
*Sweeping the clouds away.*

*I have learned life's lesson*
*Fighters who always win*
*Are those who can take it*
*Right on the chin and grin*
*So I shout to everyone:*
*Find your place in the sun,*
*Up on top of a rainbow,*
*Sweeping the clouds away!*

*Let the whole world sigh or cry*
*I'll be high in the sky,*
*Up on top of a rainbow*
*Sweeping the clouds away.*

*I don't care what's down below*
*Let the world sigh or cry*
*I'll be up on a rainbow*
*Sweeping the clouds away.*

---

FRENCH NEWSREEL, *Parade celebrating the Liberation in Clermont-Ferrand:*

Colonel Gaspar salutes General de Gaulle.

[END]

174.

August, 1944: De Gaulle on the Champs Elysées.

# APPENDIX

## A. THE MASSILIA EPISODE

After the fall of Paris on June 14, 1940, the government of the Third Republic decided to send President Lebrun, and any other members of the government who wished to pursue the struggle against Germany, on to North Africa. They were invited to travel there aboard the *Massilia*.

Admiral Darlan confirmed that deputies and senators were to leave Bordeaux aboard the *Massilia* on June 21, by order of the government. But Pierre Laval led another group of parliamentaries who opposed such a departure; Marshal Pétain congratulated those who did not wish to leave. Finally, in the confusion surrounding these contradictory maneuvers, thirty-one deputies and one senator decided to follow the President of the Republic to North Africa. At the last moment Pétain asked President Lebrun and his ministers not to go. They agreed to stay on in Bordeaux. Meanwhile the *Massilia* left Bordeaux with its crew of parliamentarians.

Negotiations for an armistice proceeded in the absence of the departed deputies; the armistice was signed on June 22. Soon the Vichy regime was denouncing the passengers of the *Massilia* and assailing their departure as "treasonous." Eight of these passengers were eventually taken prisoner, including Mendès-France; two of them were later murdered.

## B. THE BRITISH BOMBARDMENT OF MERS-EL-KEBIR

The blowing up of the French fleet at Mers-el-Kébir in Algeria seems to have been triggered by a combination of British panic, French obstinacy, and mutual distrust. Understandably alarmed by the rapid fall of France and the signing of the Franco-German armistice, the British were determined to avoid that one more powerful tool of war fall into the hands of the German juggernaut. Churchill was convinced that Hitler's word of honor had no value; he also doubted the good faith of the Vichy government. "Operation Catapult," as the British action was code-named, might well have been foreseen by the French.

Article 8 of the Armistice of June 22, 1940, read: "The French War Fleet will assemble in ports to be named later. It will be demobilized and disarmed there under German or Italian control. The German government solemnly declares to the French government that it has no intention of using the units of this Fleet in its own operations of war except however such ships as are necessary for guarding the coasts and trawling for mines."

Two days after the signing of the armistice, Admiral Darlan issued the following order to all commanders of the French Fleet: "Armistice clauses will be relayed to you elsewhere in full. I am availing myself of these last messages which I can send in code in order to tell you what I think about this matter.

1) Demobilized warships must remain French under French flag with skeleton French crew, stationed in French ports, metropolitan or colonial.

2) Secret precautions for scuttling must be taken so that neither the enemy nor foreigners who seize a ship by force can make use of it.

3) If the armistice commission charged with interpreting the armistice conditions decides otherwise than in paragraph 1, warships will, at the moment when this new decision is to be carried out and without further orders, either weigh anchor for the U.S.A. or be scuttled if they cannot otherwise escape the enemy.

4) Ships thus taken for refuge should not be used in action against Germany or Italy without the order of the Commander-in-Chief of the French sea forces."

On the same day as Darlan's order was issued, June 24th, Admiral Odendhal of the French navy mission in London wired Darlan that "The English fear to see our fleet, once disarmed, used against them." Britain and the United States continued to reproach the French government for not having sent the navy to Great Britain before appealing for an armistice. Darlan issued another order to his commanders: they were "never to obey a foreign admiralty. All ships must remain under French colors."

During the night of July 2nd to 3rd, the Royal Navy arrived in the Gulf of Oran near Mers-el-Kébir. The French fleet at Mers-el-Kébir consisted of four *cuirassiers*—the

*Dunkerque, Strasbourg, Provence,* and *Bretagne*—six destroyers, and four small destroyers. It constituted one-fifth of the entire French navy and was under the command of Admiral Gensoul.

At 7:05 A.M. Commander Holland of the Royal Navy delivered the following ultimatum to Admiral Gensoul:

"It is impossible for us, your comrades up to now, to allow your fine ships to fall into the power of the German or Italian enemy. We are determined to fight on to the end, and if we win as we think we shall, we shall never forget that France was our ally, that our interests are the same as hers, and that our common enemy is Germany. Should we conquer, we solemnly declare that we shall restore the greatness and territory of France. For this purpose we must make sure that the best ships of the French navy are not used against us by the common foe. In these circumstances His Majesty's government have instructed me to demand that the French Fleet now at Mers-el-Kébir and Oran shall act in accordance with one of the following alternatives:

a) Sail with us and continue to fight for victory against the Germans and Italians.

b) Sail with reduced crews under our control to a British port. The reduced crews will be repatriated at the earliest moment.

If either of these courses is adopted by you, we will restore your ships to France at the conclusion of the war or pay full compensation, if they are damaged meanwhile.

c) Alternatively, if you feel bound to stipulate that your ships should not be used against the Germans or Italians unless these break the Armistice, then sail with us with reduced crews to some French port in the West Indies, Martinique for instance, where they can be demilitarized to our satisfaction. Or perhaps be entrusted to the United States and remain safe until the end of the war, the crews being repatriated.

"If you refuse these fair offers, I must, with profound regret, require you to sink your ships within six hours.

"Finally, failing the above, I have the orders of His Majesty's government to use whatever force may be necessary to prevent your ships from falling into German or Italian hands."

There is much discrepancy in the accounts of what went on in the negotiations following this ultimatum. Apparently the French continued to harp on Darlan's order that they could not sail under anything but French colors. Some reports say that the third alternative offered by the British

—to sail to the French West Indies—was never discussed, or never actually transmitted to Admiral Gensoul. Other reports say the French simply refused the first two alternatives and ignored the third. Still further reports claim that the British never read aloud the final paragraphs of the ultimatum, and that the French were simply never aware of the possibility of being blown up.

After negotiating all day, Admiral Somerville of the British navy opened fire on the French fleet at 5:54 P.M. The bombardment lasted thirteen minutes and was followed by heavy attack from naval aircraft. The *Bretagne* blew up, the *Dunkerque* ran aground, the *Provence* was beached. Only the *Strasbourg* escaped. 1,297 people were killed and 351 were wounded.

Mers-el-Kébir was not an isolated attack, but part of a group of protective measures taken by the British government against the French navy. Thus, only five days after Mers-el-Kébir, the British were to blow up the battleship *Richelieu* in Dakar.

These attacks by the British produced a deep impression upon French public opinion. Vichy was to promote this anglophobia to the utmost; it seemed, after all, that England could not hold out for too long all alone against Germany. Laval was able to use the attack at Mers-el-Kébir as a pretext for abolishing the already moribund Third Republic. For, he asked, what sort of republic would base its entire foreign policy upon an alliance with the aggressors of our defenseless ships?

### C. THE RESISTANCE

Few episodes of World War II are so confusing as that of the French Resistance during the occupation. The Resistance was composed of different groups of people led by different motives. It ranged from listening to the BBC and reading underground pamphlets, to providing food and shelter for the maquisards, to spying on the Germans, to acts of sabotage and armed rebellion. Actual resistance fell more or less into three characteristic types of activity: 1) the gathering and transmission of intelligence concerning the enemy; 2) the printing and dissemination of underground newspapers and pamphlets designed to sustain a psychology of resistance; 3) sabotage of German facilities and coordination of guerilla activities with eventual Allied landings.

As early as the summer of 1940, a few individuals who refused to accept the defeat began to crystallize into little resistance groups here and there—not all or even most of which were aware of General de Gaulle in London. These groups began to print and distribute tracts and to create the framework for an effective intelligence network. Once Hitler had invaded the Soviet Union in June of 1941, the Communists, who until then had kept themselves uninvolved in the "imperialist war," became active in the Resistance. They had the advantages of iron-tight organization and experience as an underground party: they had already been outlawed in 1939 by the Third Republic for supporting the Soviet-German partition of Poland.

Resisters thus tended to fall into two main groupings: those of a conservative stripe, usually recruited from the army or the liberal middle class, and occasionally from the Church; and those of the left, predominantly Communist, mostly working class people or intellectuals. Neither of these groups, it should be noted, were particularly sympathetic to the Third Republic. The Communists formed "groupes francs,"—shock units—of about thirty men each, which came to represent the movement's secret army. By 1942 the "sabotage fer" groups involved in railroad sabotage had developed into an organization distinct from the shock units. Meanwhile on a broader level the NAP (Noyautage des administrations publiques) attempted to infiltrate the civil service with resisters.

Until the German occupation of Vichy France in November, 1942, there was a clear difference between the nature of the Resistance there and in the northern, occupied zone. Of all the Resistance movements in the southern zone, the four most important ones were:

1) Combat—Army officers and Christian Democrats under the leadership of Georges Bidault and Henri Frenzy.

2) Libération—Unionists, Communists, and Socialists under the leadership of Emmanuel d'Astier de la Vigerie.

3) Franc Tireur—Intellectuals, mostly Communists.

4) Témoignage chrétien—A Catholic group headed by a priest named Father Chaillet, one of the chief organizers of the rescue of Jewish children (who were either adopted by French families or smuggled into Switzerland). Intellectually important but comparatively small.

The capital of the Resistance in the south was Lyon. Toulouse, in the southwest corner of France, served as a smaller center of Resistance, being dominated by an organization called "Libérer et Fédérer" composed chiefly of Socialists who kept up contact with London and later formed units in the Maquis.

In April, 1943, three of the main Resistance organizations in the south—Combat, Libération, Franc Tireur—were gathered together into the MUR (Mouvements Unis de la Résistance).

In the Occupied Zone, resistance was much more dangerous from the start. But the very presence of the Germans in the north stimulated more activist reactions than in the south, which after all still had a qualified French government.

There were myriad Resistance groups in the north; almost every town had at least one local organization, even if some led very short existences. Students ran an organization called "Défense de la France." The mayor of Roubaix, near the northern coast of France, published with his socialist group a monthly called *L'homme libre*. In Paris at the Musée de l'Homme in the Palais de Chaillot, a group of young scientists, teachers, lawyers, and priests formed the "Comité de Salut public," a "Committee of Public Safety" modeled after the famous revolutionary body of 1793-94. Soon this group established contact with Britanny and the southwest of France, where their underground paper *Résistance* was first published in December 1940. In 1941 seven members of the group were executed; in 1942 two were shot, six were shot and decapitated, and others were deported to Germany.

The activities of all these groups are typical. Among the most important Resistance groups in the Occupied Zone were:

Libération-Nord—Catholics and Unionists.

Organisation civile et militaire (OCM)—Soldiers and civil servants.

Défense de la France—Students, young intellectuals.

Lorraine.

Résistance—Scientists, teachers, other professionals.

Ceux de la Libération—Group in eastern France and Paris with right-wing political opinions.

Front National—A group borrowing their ideology from the Popular Front of 1936.

After 1942 the various Resistance movements in north and south began to develop a measure of cooperation and unity. Military, political, and union organizations slowly began to spring up in the underground. Jean Moulin was sent to France from London by de Gaulle and the CNF (Comité National Français) at the beginning of 1942, with the goal of bringing some coherence to the multiple Resistance movements all over the country. On May 27, 1943, Moulin was able to officially constitute the National Resistance Council or CNR (Conseil National de la Résistance) of which he was the first president. The CNR coordinated the Maquis, the underground press, the political parties, and other Resistance movements in both the north and the south. Once Moulin was taken prisoner by the Germans in June, 1943, his role was assumed by two men: Georges Bidault, Moulin's successor and the new president of the CNR, elected by members of the Council inside France; and M. Parodi, a general delegate representing de Gaulle, who by this time was operating mostly out of North Africa.

By 1943 the Resistance movement possessed in the Maquis an impressive guerilla army. "Maquis" means a scrubby, low-lying bush found in the hills of Corsica and southern France. This type of terrain served as a comfortable refuge for all those who were fleeing the law. During the occupation the term came to be applied to those resisters who conducted their guerilla operations out of the hills in provincial France. The Maquis started in the French Alps in 1942, and in the Massif Central in 1943. Banks, post offices, and other institutions would let themselves be "robbed" by maquisards as the campaign of sabotage gained momentum. Until the end of 1943 and the first parachute drop, the Maquis had tremendous difficulty in obtaining weapons: the Allies, for fear of arming the Communists, were very reluctant to send them. Beyond the food, clothing, forged papers, and limited arms the underground network provided them, maquisards were adept at raiding the Chantiers de Jeunesse set up by Pétain and commandeering supplies.

The Maquis was very much a mixed group. The units varied in size, efficiency, and politics. Jews, refugees, anti-Franco Spanish revolutionaries, and even a few left-wing Germans fought in the Maquis. But the impetus which transformed the Maquis into a veritable army was the institution in February 1943 of compulsory labor laws, the STO (Service du Travail Obligatoire). These laws required all young Frenchmen to work directly under the Germans either in Germany or in German-controlled factories inside France. The laws directly affected the everyday life of many thousands and threatened the lives of millions. Effectively, those who did not wish to join up and work for the Germans were forced to flee into active Resistance. The number of deserters from the STO was approximately 100,000.

By the beginning of 1944 the sporadic guerilla warfare of the Maquis could be developed into more organized military activity. The CNR had already formed for itself a "Comité d'action militaire" to coordinate strategy; on February 1, 1944, all guerilla and sabotage activities were combined into the French interior forces, the FFI (Forces Françaises de l'Intérieur). The FFI served as a catch-all for Resistance forces in the months preceding the liberation.

Within the FFI, the Communists created their own group called the "Francs Tireurs et Partisans" (FTP). There was also the "Milice Patriotique", a paramilitary Communist group.

## FRENCH GOVERNMENTS SINCE 1940

*Third Republic*

Paul Reynaud, Premier. March 21, 1940 to June 17, 1940.

Philippe Pétain, Premier. June 17, 1940 to July 11, 1940.

*French State (Vichy)*

Philippe Pétain, Head of State.

Pierre Laval, Vice President of the Cabinet. July 12, 1940 to December 13, 1940.

François Darlan, Pierre Etienne Flandin, and General Huntziger, Members of the "Comité directeur" of the government. December 14, 1940 to February 9, 1941.

François Darlan, Vice President of the Cabinet. February 10, 1941 to April 17, 1942.

Pierre Laval, Head of the Government. April 18, 1942 to September, 1944. At the end of 1943 Darnand, Déat and Henriot are forced upon Laval by the Germans.

*Provisional Government of the French Republic*

Charles de Gaulle, President. June 3, 1944 (in Algeria) to September 9, 1944 (in Paris), and up until January 20, 1946.

Succession of provisional heads while the constitution of the first constituent assembly is rejected by a referendum: Félix Gouin, January 1946 to June 1946; Georges Bidault June to November 1946; Léon Blum December 1946 to January 1947.

*Fourth Republic*

January 22, 1947 to January 8, 1959.

*Fifth Republic*

January 8, 1959—

## CHRONOLOGY 1939-1945

**1939.**

April. Lebrun re-elected President.

August 21. Soviet–German agreement announced.

August 22. French Communist party supports Soviet-German agreement.

September 1. Germany invades Poland.

September 3. France and Great Britain declare war on Germany.

September 17. USSR invades Poland.

September 26. Prime Minister Daladier dissolves the French Communist Party.

September 28. Moscow agreements leading to partition of Poland between USSR and Germany.

November 4. USA Neutrality Act.

December 14. USSR expelled from League of Nations.

**1940.**

March 20. Reynaud succeeds Daladier as Prime Minister.

March 28. French–British agreement not to conclude a separate peace.

May 10. Germany invades the Netherlands.

May 13–14. French front broken on Meuse.

May 18–19. Cabinet shuffle: Reynaud takes over Defense Ministry from Daladier, Weygand replaces Gamelin. Pétain enters government as Secretary of State and Vice-President of the Cabinet.

May 29–June 4. Evacuation at Dunkirk.

June 10. French government moves to Tours. Italy declares war on France and Great Britain.

June 11. Churchill, Eden, and Pétain meet at Briare.

June 14. Germans enter Paris. French government moves to Bordeaux.

June 15. Hitler's early morning visit to Paris.

June 16. Reynaud resigns; Pétain becomes Prime Minister. Pétain asks Germans for an armistice.

June 17. De Gaulle leaves for London with General Spears.

June 18. De Gaulle calls from London for continued resistance against Germany.

June 21. The *Massilia* leaves Bordeaux for Morocco.

June 22. French–German armistice signed at Rethondes.

June 24. French–Italian armistice.

June 28. Great Britain recognizes de Gaulle as leader of the Free French.

July 2. French government settles in Vichy.

July 3. British sink the French fleet at Mers-el-Kébir.

July 4. Diplomatic relations between Vichy and Great Britain severed.

July 8. British blow up the *Richelieu* in Dakar.

July 10. French parliament in Vichy votes 569–80 to give full powers to Marshal Pétain.

July 11. Vote on constitutional laws abolishes the Third Republic and creates in its place the "French State." Laval becomes Pétain's head minister.

July 30. Legislation creates the Chantiers de Jeunesse.

September. Free French expedition to Dakar fails to rouse French North Africa.

October 24. Hitler and Pétain meet at Montoire.

December 13. Laval dismissed. Flandin as interim minister.


**1941.**

February. Admiral Darlan takes control of government.

June 22. Germany invades USSR. French Communists begin Resistance.

June 30. Diplomatic relations between Vichy and the Soviet Union severed.

September 24. Formation of Comité National de la France Libre.

1942

January 1. Jean Moulin, representative of de Gaulle and the Comité National Français (CNF), parachutes into unoccupied France.

April. Trial of Blum, Daladier, and other ministers of the Third Republic becomes embarrassing to Vichy regime and is abandoned. Laval returns to power.

May 1. U.S. Ambassador leaves Vichy.

May 29. Jews in the Occupied Zone are required to wear yellow star.

July 16. "Vél d'Hiv Round-up": 4,000 Jewish children arrested by Parisian police.

July 21. 22,000 Jews are arrested in Paris.

November 8. Allied invasion of North Africa. Darlan, in Algeria, switches to support the Allies.

November 11. Germans occupy Vichy France.

December 24. Darlan assassinated. Giraud succeeds him as military commander in North Africa.


1943

January. Casablanca Conference including Roosevelt, Churchill, de Gaulle, and Giraud.

January 30. French Militia formed under Joseph Darnand.

February 16. Institution of compulsory labor (STO).

April. Formation in the south of the United Movements of the Resistance (MUR).

May 15. Formation of the National Resistance Council (CNR).

June 3. Formation of the Committee of National Liberation (CFLN) in Algiers under de Gaulle and Giraud.

June 21. Jean Moulin taken prisoner. Georges Bidault becomes president of the CNR.

September. Liberation of Corsica.


1944.

January. Crisis in Vichy government. Collaborationists from Paris—Déat, Darnand, Henriot—enter government.

March 27. Vichy law authorizing the French to join the Waffen S.S.

June 3. De Gaulle becomes president of the French Provisional Government.

June 6. Allied landing in Normandy.

June 9. Forces of the interior Resistance (FFI) integrated into the French Army.

July 10. De Gaulle meets Roosevelt.

August 15. French and American armies in Provence.

August 20. Germans transfer Pétain to Belfort.

August 25. Liberation of Paris.

August 26. De Gaulle enters Paris.

September. Pétain and Laval installed at Sigmaringen Castle.

October 4. Reorganization of courts to facilitate prosecution of "collaborators."

October 5. Women's suffrage.

October 22. Allies recognize the Provisional French Government.


1945.

October 21. Referendum brings official end to the Third Republic. Constituent assembly convened.

## GLOSSARY OF NAMES AND ORGANIZATIONS

*Action Française*: French royalist organization (and newspaper of same name) known for extreme political and social conservatism and for advocacy of the violent overthrow of the Third Republic. Its most influential spokesman was Charles Maurras.

*Actualités Mondiales*: French newsreels.

*Auvergne*: Province in south central France whose principal city is Clermont-Ferrand.

*Léon Blum*: Prominent French politician and writer. As Socialist leader of the Popular Front government he served as Prime Minister from June 1936 to June 1937, and for one month in 1938. His Jewish background made him a prime target for the anti-Semitic right.

*Bobet*: Champion cyclist.

*Boche*: Slang for a German.

*Brinon, Fernand de*: Pétain's "ambassador" to the Germans in Paris, a financier and political go-between well at home in the shady world of collaborationist Paris.

*Buchenwald*: Concentration camp from 1937 to 1945, located northeast of Weimar in Saxony.

*Charlemagne division*: Name given the French unit of the Waffen S.S.

*Chevalier de la Légion d'Honneur*: The Légion d'Honneur is an order of high distinction and reward for civil and military services originated by Napoleon. Being named "chevalier" is basically the equivalent of being knighted.

*Chantiers de Jeunesse*: Rural work camps for French youth, created by Marshal Pétain after the Armistice as a substitute for military service. The activities were not dissimilar to those in the New Deal's Civilian Conservation Corps, though Vichy leaders tried to use the camps as forums to instill traditional rural values in the young.

*Chateaubriand, Alphonse de*: A French writer of novels and short stories who received the prix Goncourt in 1911. In

1937 he became a National-Socialist, and during the occupation a fervent collaborator. He founded the newspaper *La Gerbe* and served as president of the group "Collaboration."

*Chleu*: Slang for a person of German nationality.

*CNR (Conseil National de la Résistance, National Resistance Council)*: Group founded by Jean Moulin in May 1943 to coordinate Resistance activities in north and south of France. See Appendix C.

*Darquier de Pellepoix*: A rabid anti-Semite, active in Action Française, who succeeded Xavier Vallat as the General Commissioner for Jewish Affairs.

*De Gaulle*: During his service from 1932 to 1936 in the Supreme Defense Council, de Gaulle attempted unsuccessfully to convince French military chiefs of the need for tanks and motorized forces in modern warfare. He served in the Reynaud cabinet of 1940 as Under-Secretary of Defense, coordinating British and French military activities, before leaving for England upon Pétain's accession to power.

*Doriot, Jacques*: A Communist leader from the working class suburb of St. Dénis from 1924 to 1934, he did an abrupt aboutface after the disturbances of 1934 and in 1936 founded the fascist Parti Populaire Français. One of the most violent of the Paris collaborators.

*Drumont, Edouard*: Nineteenth century French politician and writer known as a bitter anti-Semite. His book *La France juive* of 1886, attacking Jews and republicans, helped to stir up reactions during the Dreyfus Affair.

*FFI (Forces Françaises de l'Intérieur)*: Resistance forces inside France. See Appendix C.

*francisque*: Hatchet used by the ancient Gauls and Francs, borrowed by the Vichy government as a symbol of tradition and feudal values.

*Freemason*: Member of the secret society known for intellectual rationalism and an anticlerical stance. Often persecuted in French history.

*FTP (Franc Tireurs et Partisans)*: Resistance group of Communist tendency. See Appendix C.

*Free French (Forces Françaises libres)*: Forces outside metropolitan France who actively took part in the war against Germany despite the armistice.

*Gauleiter*: Direct representative of the Führer.

*Gestapo (GEheime STAatsPOlizei)*: Nazi state police, organized by Hermann Goering in 1933.

*le grand Jules*: "big Julius," French nickname for Hitler.

*Gringoire*: French newspaper of pro-Fascist, anti-Semitic, anti-British accent.

*Heydrich, Reinhard*: Called "Heydrich der Henker" ("Heydrich the Executioner"), he was a Nazi politician, an assistant to Himmler noted for his effective elimination of German Communists and the terrorization of Czechs after 1938. He was assassinated in Prague in 1942.

*Himmler, Heinrich*: Organizer of the SS, paramilitary Nazi party organization.

*l'Humanité*: French Communist Party newspaper.

*Huntziger, General Charles*: French army officer and politician, signer of the June 22 armistice. He served as Pétain's minister of war until he died in a plane crash in 1941.

*Iron cross*: German military decoration.

*Jerusalem artichokes*: One of the only available foods in Vichy France.

*Laval, Pierre*: Laval began his political career as a leftwing deputy from the Paris working class suburb of Aubervilliers. In 1926 he slowly started moving to the right, serving as Prime Minister a number of times before 1940. Although often portrayed as a Germanophile and ardent collaborator, some sincerely believe he tried to ward off the German influence, at least in Vichy. It is certain that he was not pleased when the Germans imposed Darnand and Déat upon him in early 1944. After the Liberation he was tried for treason, sentenced to death and shot. His role in French history remains highly ambiguous.

*Lorraine Squadron*: The French unit within the Royal Air Force.

*Maginot Line*: Group of fortifications built on French eastern frontier between 1927 and 1936.

*Maquis, maquisard*: Guerilla resistance fighters operating outside urban areas. See Appendix C.

*Massilia*: See Appendix A.

*Mélisse*: Prison of the French Militia.

*Mers-el-Kébir*: See Appendix B.

*Milice, milicien*: The French Militia, a paramilitary organization created by the Vichy government in January 1943 under the aegis of Joseph Darnand. The Militia collaborated enthusiastically with the Germans and was particularly effective in picking off members of the Resistance.

*Montoire*: Meeting place of Pétain and Hitler in October, 1940.

*National Resistance Council*: See CNR.

*New Europe*: Term used to connote a united Europe under Fascist control; part of Fascism's attempt to portray itself as a modern, "revolutionary" movement with historical significance.

*Occupied Zone (Zone occupée)*: That part of France, including Paris, occupied by the Germans according to the armistice of June 22. See map on page 4.

*Pétain, Philippe*: Head of Vichy France and Commander-in-Chief of the French army during part of World War I. Noted for successful defense of Verdun in 1916. Previous to becoming Head of State, he served as France's ambassador to Franco Spain.

*poilu*: French soldier.

*le Populaire*: Left-wing newspaper, official organ of the French Socialist Party.

*Popular Front*: Term describing the working alliance of French parties opposed to Fascism, both Communist and non-Communist, an alliance which came into being in the 1930's. The Popular Front first gained power with Léon Blum as Premier in 1936 but, torn by internal dissension, it was succeeded by the more conservative government of Edouard Daladier.

*PPF (Parti Populaire Français)*: The French Fascist Party led by Jacques Doriot.

*Rabat*: Administrative capital of French Morocco; seaport.

*RAF*: British Royal Air Force.

*Reynaud, Paul*: French premier during the invasion and fall of France, he negotiated the agreement with Great Britain barring a separate armistice with Germany, and resigned after Pétain insisted on calling for one on June 16, 1940.

*Rokossovsky*: Russian-Polish commander who broke through the Eastern Front against German forces. Later he served as Vice-Premier of Poland.

*Saint-Cyr*: French military academy, roughly equivalent to West Point.

*SOE*: Secret Operations Executive. The British espionage network.

*Speer, Albert ("Professor Speer")*: Economic advisor to Hitler, author of *Inside the Third Reich*.

*S.S.*: (*Schutz-Staffel*) Paramilitary Nazi Party organization founded in 1929 by Heinrich Himmler. With it Hitler was able to liquidate Röhm and the S.A.(Sturm-Abteilung) in 1934. By 1940 it had become an official military organization, renamed the Waffen S.S.

*STO (Service du Travail Obligatoire)*: Compulsory labor under the Germans.

*Unoccupied Zone (Zone libre)*: Vichy France. See map on p. 4.

*Victor of Verdun*: Marshal Pétain.

*Waffen S.S.*: Name given the S.S. after 1940, once it had become incorporated into the official German military. The Waffen S.S. was charged with running concentration camps and, with the Gestapo, of surveillance in the occupied territories.

*Wehrmacht*: Term used for the whole of German land, sea, and air forces.

*Weygand, General Maxime*: Commander in Chief of French forces at the time of the defeat in 1940. He served under the Vichy government, for which he was later tried and cleared.

*Work, Family, Fatherland (Travail, Patrie, Famille)*: The slogan which typified Vichy political philosophy; it was upon these three pillars that a new, anti-democratic, semi-corporate state was to be built.

*Zay, Jean*: French political leader and lawyer, minister of education in the Popular Front government of 1936 and through to 1939. He was arrested by the Vichy government on charges stemming from the *Massilia* incident, and assassinated by the French Militia in June, 1944.